CW01660248

THE JEWS IN THE C
DURING THE GERMAN OCCUPATION
1940-1945

by

FREDERICK COHEN
President of the Jersey Jewish Congregation

(Front cover photograph Therese Steiner)

Published by
Jersey Heritage Trust
Pier Road, St Helier, Jersey JE2 3NF

in association with
The Institute of Contemporary History and Wiener Library Limited
4 Devonshire Street, London W1N 2BH

Second Edition published 2000

© Frederick Cohen 2000

All rights reserved

Jersey
Heritage Trust

Part 1 was first published in the September 1997 edition of 'The Journal of Holocaust Education', published by Frank Cass and Company Limited

A French translation of Part 1 was included in the Jan-April 2000 edition of 'Revue d'Histoire de la Shoal Le Monde Juif' published by the Centre de Documentation Juive Contemporaine, Paris.

Parts 1 (revised) and Part 2 were published by the Institute of Contemporary History and Wiener Library Limited in association with the Jersey Jewish Congregation in 1998 to complement the Synagogue memorial service held in September 1998

Albert Gustave Bedane 1893-1980

Recognised by the State of Israel as

'Righteous Among The Nations'

for his heroism in hiding
Mrs Richardson in Jersey from 1943-1945

To the memory of

Marianne Grunfeld
Auguste Spitz
Therese Steiner

and those of all nationalities and religions who suffered during the German Occupation of the Channel islands

'Remember the past,
Live for the present,
Hope for the future'

Abba Kovner, 1918–1987
Hebrew poet and resistance fighter in the Vilna ghetto

Contents

Foreword

This documentary paper on the Channel Islands under Nazi occupation during the War, with special reference to the Jewish community, is thoroughly researched and deeply moving and an important contribution to Holocaust literature.

The author is to be congratulated on his painstaking research, opening an invaluable insight into a relatively new department of Holocaust literature.

The material should prove useful to Holocaust historians and researchers, and be of enormous practical use especially to Jewish schools and Holocaust departments at universities the world over.

This darkest chapter of Jewish history may now be over half a century old, but its documentation and its relevance to future attitudes by Jews and non-Jews alike becomes ever more vital, especially in understanding the mystique of Jewish survival and reconstruction.

Lord Immanuel Jakobovits
Emeritus Chief Rabbi

Appreciation

The author wishes to express his sincere thanks to a number of individuals.
Joe Miere the retired curator of the German Underground Hospital in Jersey has steadfastly endeavoured to record for posterity the details of all those who suffered during the Occupation, for whatever reason, regardless of their nationality or religion. He has collected a substantial Occupation archive and all those who study this period owe him an incalculable debt of gratitude for his strenuous and determined efforts over so many years.
Richard Heaume, the owner of the German Occupation Museum and Major Edwin Parks a reporter at the Guernsey Evening Press have also made key contributions to recording the fate of the Jews in Guernsey and both made their archives available to the author.
William Bell of Guernsey also has made a significant contribution to recording the fate of the Guernsey resident Jews and provided willing assistance to the author.
John Noel of the Jersey Immigration Department devoted time and effort in researching the Aliens Office archives.
Annie Dolan and Henny Prax in Jersey and Zittora Raphael in Israel, provided detailed translations of French, German and Hebrew documents. Paul Saunders in Cambridge provided invaluable advice and translated numerous German documents. Wayne Audrain designed the cover of this edition at very short notice.
Advocate Anita Regal and Bob Le Sueur in Jersey, and Brian Bonnard in Alderney provided valuable advice on sections of the text. Stephen Stodel in London and David Feldman in Jersey kindly assisted with proof reading
The Esther Pauline Lloyd diaries are now held in the collection of the Wiener Library
Acknowledgement for the photographs and images are due to Yad Vashem, the Wiener Library, the Jersey Archive Service, The Guernsey Archive Service, Richard Heaume, the Jersey Evening Post, Joe Miere and the family of Samuel Simon.
The author also wishes to thank: Elisabeth Bois, Jersey; Brian Bonnard, Alderney; Frederick Brown, Jersey; Madeleine Bunting, London; Albert Chardine, Jersey; Lorraine and Advocate Richard Falle, Jersey; Peter Hassall, Canada; Olga Ozouf, Jersey; Stella Perkins, Jersey; Iris Prigent, Jersey; Bob Sowden, Jersey; The Guernsey Archive Service, particularly Dr Darryl Ogier; The Jersey Archive Service, particularly Denise Williams and Catherine Burke; The Archives of the Conseil General de la Mayenne; The Lord Coutanche Societe Jersiaise Library; Yad Vashem Archive, Israel, particularly Zvi Bernhardt; The Bundesarchiv Military archives; The Centre de Documentation Juive Contemporaine, Paris.
Lastly and very specially to Dr Jo Reilly of the Institute of Contemporary History and Wiener Library in London who assisted with research and advised on content and presentation.

Part 1

Jewish residents of the Channel Islands during the German Occupation

Jewish residents of the Channel Islands during the German Occupation

Introduction

The Holocaust, perhaps the greatest evil of the twentieth century, was perpetrated against the Jewish people in Europe between 1933 and 1945. It was authored by Hitler's Nazi ideology and implemented by the German war machine. It was also made possible by the complicity of administrations throughout Europe under German occupation. The Channel Islands, the only parts of the British Isles occupied by the Germans between 1940 and 1945, were not untouched by this. The impact of that Occupation on those *'deemed to be Jews'*, and the chronicle of the relationship between the German occupation authorities and the local civil administration form a small but important part of the Holocaust as a whole. This issue has received a minor consideration so far in the wide range of historical and biographical publications made about the Occupation of the Channel Islands. To some extent this has been because most detailed documentary evidence has only recently become available.

The function of this monograph is limited. It aims to present the evidence now available, on the triangular relationship between the German occupying power, the local civilian insular administrators and those who suffered in the Channel Islands because they were *'deemed to be Jews'*. It is presented as a source of information rather than as a historical analysis. Its role is not to make judgements, assign responsibilities or to draw final conclusions.

Earlier versions of this paper

This paper was first published in the *Journal of Holocaust Education* in 1997. A French translation of the paper was included in the Jan-April 2000 edition of 'Revue d'Histoire de la Shoal Le Monde Juif' published by the Centre de Documentation Juive Contemporaine, Paris.

The text was revised in 1998 for inclusion in a commemorative volume to complement the memorial service held at the Jersey Synagogue in memory of the Jews who suffered in the islands.

In 2000 the text has again been revised to incorporate the information contained in the Jersey Attorney-General's wartime file 'Law Officers Department, Jersey - Jewish Undertakings Etc' uncovered in 1999.

Sources

Many sources, either previously unavailable, unpublished or unresearched in relation to this subject have been examined.

In 1995 the author uncovered the civilian authorities file 'Aliens Office, Island of Jersey, Orders relating to Measures against the Jews' in a dusty cardboard box in the archive of the Greffier of the States of Jersey. This file made national headlines and provided the first real insight into the day-to-day implementation of the Orders against the Jews in Jersey.[1]

In 1996 numerous files comprising British Military Intelligence reports and governmental correspondence were released by the Public Records Office in London. The release was widely covered in the national press and many of these documents together with others at the PRO provide useful information on post-war interpretation of the implementation of the anti-Jewish measures in the islands.[2]

One hundred files of the wartime Law Officers Department emerged in 1999 during the move of the department to new building. These files detail the operational relationship between the civilian authorities and the German occupiers on matters from anti-Jewish legislation and policing, to agriculture and post-war inquiries. Many of these files significantly enhance our understanding of the process of government and policing during the Occupation. Of these files, the Jersey Attorney-General's file 'Jewish Undertakings etc' provides new insight into the process of the *Aryanization* of Jewish businesses and the search for undeclared Jews.

Two Jersey Aliens Office diaries not previously examined contain references to Jewish residents and the process of routing out undeclared Jews. The first is entitled 'Registration and Identification of Persons (Jersey) Order 1940' and covers the period January 1941 to October 1942.[3] The second volume is a more general office diary covering the period from December 1940 until after the liberation.

The Esther Pauline Lloyd diaries uncovered by the author in 1997 are now in the archive of the Wiener Library. The two surviving volumes provide a unique day-by-day account of the experiences of a registered

[1] Jersey Archive Service (JAS), Aliens Office, Island of Jersey - Order relating to measures against Jews, GEN/3/1940; The Guardian, April 1995, p.1.

[2] The Times 20 Nov 1996, The Telegraph 18 Nov 1996, Daily mail 20,23 Nov 1996

[3] Clifford Orange was appointed Chief Registration Officer under the Registration and Identification of Persons (Jersey) Order, 1940.

British Jew deported from Jersey in 1943 firstly to Compiegne internment camp in France and then to Biberach in Germany.

A file of papers held at the Yad Vashem archive in Jerusalem provides significant information on the implementation of the measures against the Jews in Guernsey. This file contains many papers originating from the Bailiff and Controlling Committee's offices. The file also includes correspondence between the Feldkommandantur in Jersey and Guernsey and their superiors on the European mainland concerning the registration of the Yellow Star order and the deportation of many of the islands' Jews.[4] It is not known who sent these documents to Yad Vashem although some were clearly copied from the files of the various departments of the States of Guernsey.

Other surviving files of both the Feldkommandantur and the Controlling Committee are held at the Guernsey Archive Service. An important file is held at the Guernsey Greffier's office containing documents relating to the registration and implementation of the various orders against the Jews in the island.

The unpublished diaries of the Reverend Douglas Ord at the Priaulx Library in Guernsey represent perhaps the most detailed and extensive chronology of the German occupation and contain a number of references relevant to both the island's Jews and forced workers.

Other significant relevant documents were found in the archives of the Centre de Documentation Juive Contemporaine, the Bundesarchiv Military Archive, the Berlin Document Centre, the archives of the Conseil General de la Mayenne, Yad Vashem, the Nationalmuseet of Denmark, the Moscow State Archive and in the private collections of a number of Channel Islanders.

The Jewish community in the Channel Islands before the Occupation

There has been a Jewish community in Jersey since the early nineteenth century and a synagogue was built in 1842 at 100 Halkett Place, St Helier. Although the synagogue had ceased to be used by the end of the century, those Jewish families remaining on the island had continued to hold religious services in private houses and lived openly as Jews. Two Jewish cemeteries, both dating from the nineteenth century, existed in St Helier, the oldest an enclosed cemetery at Westmont, and the second a part of the Almorah all-denominational cemetery. Neither cemetery was

---

[4] The Controlling Committee was formed by the States of Guernsey in 1940 to deal with matters concerning the German occupying authorities. Jurat the Rev. John Leale was President from Oct 1940. The equivalent body in Jersey was the Superior Council presided over by the Bailiff, Alexander M. Coutanche.

desecrated by the Germans although the Jewish headstones at Almorah were laid flat during the Occupation.[5]

The majority of the well-established practising Jews resident in Jersey left the island before June 1940. An incomplete list of many of those who had left the island was compiled by Clifford Orange the Chief Aliens Officer and sent to the German authorities on 6 January 1942.[6] The Passport Office lists show that many members of the families named by Orange renewed their passports in the months leading up to the Occupation. The last to do so was Rose Rachel Feldman who obtained her new passport on 15 June 1940. The passport office closed on 27 June 1940.[7]

Jews were first noted in Guernsey in the 1760's but no synagogue is known to have been built. Although no formal Jewish community existed in Guernsey a number of Jews including Dr William Montague, Louis Cohen, David Rudnidsky, and Mr and Mrs William Middlewick had evacuated from the island before the German occupation.[8]

The Jersey and Guernsey Jewish families were well aware of the danger the approaching German forces posed to them. Considerable information was available locally on the anti-Jewish measures being implemented in Europe before the war. In the months of January and February 1939 alone the 'Jersey Evening Post' printed more than 15 articles detailing the anti-Semitic measures then being implemented on the Continent.

During the Occupation, Professor Karl Heinz Pfeffer, Head of the Great Britain Department in the Faculty of Foreign Studies at Berlin University was sent to the islands by the German occupying forces to compile a report.[9] One section of his report was clearly written in line with Berlin's anti-Semitic policy to revile Jewish practices in relation to the slaughtering of animals. This section however provides an important indication of the Bailiff of Jersey's awareness of the interests of the pre-war Jewish Community. The relevant section noted:

---

[5] A. Regal, 'History of the Jersey Jewish Community', unpublished manuscript; the Westmount Cemetery was purchased by the Jersey Jewish Community in 1836 and remains in use today.

[6] Island of Jersey, Aliens Office (AO), Orders relating to measures against Jews, GEN/3/1940. Clifford Orange listed: Israel Cohen; Phineas Cohen; Louis Feldman; Catherine Pauline Hill; Jack Moss Israel; Alfred Krichefski; Wilfred Krichefski; Dudley Marks; Elizabeth Marks; Harry Leopold Marks; Simon Peretz; Rebecca Peretz; Sidney Podro; Mina Podro; William Rosenberg; Beryl Silver; and Blanche Silver.

[7] See Jersey Immigration Department (JID), Passport lists.

[8] Rev Douglas Ord diaries Oct 1940; Frank Falla, The Silent War (Guernsey, 1967), p.20; Yad Vashem (YV), papers on Guernsey Series 0.9.

[9] Report on a study visit to the Channel Islands 10 - 25 Sept. 1941 Guernsey Archive Service (GAS), File FK 5-6.

> *'The Bailiff of Jersey, also head of state, received us in a very correct manner and as we were feeling our way to the question on the functioning of the ancient constitution in a modern context, he replied that things were working fine. As an example he cited that he had enforced a specific law on painless slaughtering in Jersey as the first country of the Empire. However, subsequently a Jewish interests envoy from England had paid him a visit and demanded an exception for ritual slaughter.*
>
> *As a decent Christian [the Bailiff is reported as saying] I instantly came to an agreement with this decent Jew and allowed an exception, of which only little practical use was made. You can see how a decent Christian can intercourse with a decent Jew, even under a seemly ancient constitution.'*[10]

The Aliens Office in the period leading up to the outbreak of war had been involved in regulating the movement of aliens arriving in the islands for any purpose. In 1938 and early 1939 a number of Jews from Germany applied to reside in Jersey to escape persecution. A number of the letters from the applicants, including a very detailed letter from the Nimptsch family, contain descriptions of the persecution being suffered by Jews in Germany at that time. The Bailiff, Alexander Coutanche and the Chief Aliens Officer, Clifford Orange handled the applications and in each case a submission was made to the Defence Committee. Decisions were taken with reference to Home Office guidelines.[11]

Despite the financial independence of some applicants and, in the case of Mrs Nimptsch, the support of Clifford Orange, the Defence Committee transmitted its rejection of all the applications from German Jews to the Bailiff. However, permission to come to the islands was granted to Charles Rosenberg, a Turkish Jew, although confirmation that he ultimately arrived in the islands has not been established.[12] Charles Rosenberg's application was sponsored by Nathan Davidson, who during

---

[10] The Bailiffs of Jersey and Guernsey together with the Attorney-General and Solicitor General are appointed by the English Crown. The Bailiff of Jersey is head of the legislature, head of the judiciary and first citizen; The Statute referred to was Betail Etranger, Viande de Boucherie et Abatage 1933 to which an amendment was passed in 1934 allowing Jewish slaughtering practices. This amendment was passed when Alexander Coutanche was still Attorney-General; he became Bailiff in 1935.

[11] JID, file, States Greffe Department – German nationals and German nationals professing Jewish faith; Jersey Archive Service (JAS), Statutory Rules and Orders relating to Aliens 1920, Bailiff of Jersey files BA/W/4/3&1.

[12] Permission was also granted by the Jersey and Guernsey authorities to four Austrian born women and a Pole to live and work in the Islands. These women registered as Jews in Oct. 1940 during the Occupation; JID, file, States Greffe Department – Turkish nationals and Turkish nationals professing Jewish faith.

the German occupation was to become one of the registered Jews in Jersey.

In accordance with policy in England enemy aliens were interned before the Occupation for a short period from the end of May until the end of June 1940. Amongst those interned in Guernsey were three women who were subsequently registered as Jews under the orders of the German occupying forces in October 1940. Theresa Steiner and Auguste Spitz were both born in Austria and interned 4 June 1940. Annie Wranowsky, a Czech resident in Sark who was assumed to be a German national, was interned on 1 June.[13] All three were released by 25 June. In Jersey male enemy aliens were interned on 26 May including Hans Hurban the Austrian born Gentile husband of Margarete Hurban, who in October 1940 registered as Jewish in Jersey. Hans Hurban was released on 21 June.[14]

The German Military administration of the Channel Islands

The German occupation began in Guernsey on 30 June 1940, in Jersey on 1 July, in Alderney on 2 July, and in Sark on 3 July. By August 1940 the occupiers had begun to turn their attention to identifying foreign Jews still resident in the islands.[15]

Occupied France was divided into four areas of military government, with headquarters in Paris. The Channel Islands formed part of 'Zone A' (North-West France) and civilian affairs orders originating in Paris were received via St Germain-en-Laye where necessary adaptations were made. The civil affairs department of the German military government of the Channel Islands was operated by Feldkommandantur 515 in Jersey. The Feldkommandantur was responsible for the smooth running of the civilian affairs of the islands and for bringing the policies of the islands in line with those dictated by Germany. The first Feldkommandant, Colonel Schumacher, was followed in September

[13] Guernsey Archive Service (GAS), File CC 3-20, Report to Dr Brosch 2 Oct. 1940 including summary of internment procedures at Fort Houmet by Dep. Inspector A. Longmead. Annie Wranowsky was incorrectly assumed to be German at the time as she possessed a Judenpass (No. 558) issued in London on 13 Feb. 1939 and she may have obtained early release from internment.

[14] See Jersey Evening Post, 27 May 1940; JAS, Bailiff of Jersey files BA/W/4/3&1; JID, List of German Internees.

[15] Charles Chruickshank, The German Occupation of the Channel Islands (Guernsey, 1991, 8th ed.), p.74. He states that the Occupation of Sark began on 4 July 1940 but most other accounts state the previous day; GAS, File CC 3-20 Letter dated 24 August 1940 from President of Controlling Committee to Inspector of Police stating the request of the Feldkommandantur for information on the religion of every alien.

1941 by Colonel Knackfuss. Schumacher established a subordinate office in Guernsey, the Nebenstelle, also responsible for policy in Sark.[16]

Oberkriegsverwaltungsrat (OKVR) Dr Gottfreid Von Stein was appointed as Chief Administrator of the German occupation government of the Channel Islands at Feldkommandantur 515 in Jersey[17], responsible for economic measures, provision of food, policing, liaison with German High Command in Paris and the implementation of anti-Jewish policies. Von Stein was succeeded in August 1941 by OKVR Dr Wilhelm Casper. On 10 November 1943 Dr Casper was transferred from the island and Baron Hans Max von Aufsess, previously his deputy, was promoted to Chief Administrator. Kriegsverwaltungsrat (KVR) Dr Brosch was appointed senior administrator at the Nebenstelle in Guernsey. Dr Casper and Dr Brosch had both been civilian lawyers before the war.

The civilian authorities such as the Bailiff's Office and the Aliens Office primarily corresponded with the staff of the Feldkommandantur rather than the military staff of the Wehrmacht and thus much of the surviving documentation relating to the implementation of the measures against the Jews is contained in the files of FK 515 and the civilian authorities.

The German administrators in Jersey and Guernsey, many of whose names or departments appear in correspondence relating to the measures against the islands Jews, together with their administrative duties, as at 8 Aug. 1942 were listed as follows:[18]

> Jersey:
> Oberst Knackfuss, Head of military section.
> OKVR Dr Casper, Chief non-military administrator – Personnel – Local civilian authorities.
> KVR Dr Reffler, General administration – Financial affairs.
> KVR Frhr v Aufsess, Industrial economy.
> KVR Peltz, Agriculture and food.
> Sdf (z) Herzog, Assistant to other departments listed above.
>
> Guernsey:
> KVR Dr Brosh, Head of administration and military section – Finance – Labour – Social issues.
> KVI Zachau, Economy – Transport – Assistant to motor transport department – Non military supply and provisions.
> An earlier list of 7 June 1941 details the Nebenstelle administrators as follows.
> Rittmeister Fuerst von Oettingen, Command.
> KVR Dr Reffler, Head of administration - Food and agriculture.
> KVI Zachau, Policing – Provisions - Fuel and transport.
> Lt. John, Feldgendarmerie.

[16] Chruickshank, The German Occupation, pp.104-7.

[17] Dr W. J. Casper, Remembrances from the Channel Islands 1941-1943, (Jersey, 1991). p.114.

[18] GAS, File FK 5-6.

KVR Dr Brosch does not appear on this list but it is clear from the correspondence with the Controlling Committee that he was dealing with some matters concerning Aliens and Jews by October 1940.

The Orders against the Jews registered in the Islands Royal Courts

The implementation of the discriminatory measures against the Jews remaining in the Channel Islands commenced on Monday, 21 October 1940 when the following notice appeared in the 'Jersey Evening Post':

> *JEWS TO REGISTER*
>
> *The Bailiff said he had received two Orders from the German authorities, the first relating to measures to be taken for the registration of Jews. This was read by the Attorney-General and on his conclusions was lodged au Greffe and its promulgation ordered.*
>
> *The Bailiff announced that he had entrusted the Chief Aliens Officer with the registration of the Jews under the Order.*

The measures implemented against the Jews of the Channel Islands comprised formal orders originating from Paris. The orders mirrored the pattern of orders and measures against the Jews in France. These orders were subsequently registered in the Royal Courts of Jersey and Guernsey by the civilian authorities under instruction from the occupying German authorities. Dr William Casper stated, in relation to the general orders emanating from the Military Commander in France, that '*the Chief Administrator for the islands could in theory make exceptions if he felt the orders weren't applicable locally*'.

On 8 July 1940 the German commander, Captain Gussek, after consultation with the Bailiff of Jersey, issued a proclamation that was to form the basis of the legal relations between the civilian authorities and the German occupiers. This stated,

> *'The Civil Government and Courts of the Island will continue to function as heretofore save that all Laws, Ordinances, Regulations and Orders will be submitted to the German Commandant before being enacted....*
>
> *The Orders of the German Commandant heretofore now and hereafter issued shall in due course be registered in the records*

> *of the Island of Jersey, in order that no person may plead ignorance thereof.'*[19]

The early Orders against the Jews were published in the 'Jersey Evening Post' and the 'Guernsey Evening Press'. The Feldkommandant determined that the later orders were to be registered in the Royal Courts but not advertised in the local newspaper, registered Jews were to be informed directly of the terms of each order. As an example, Clifford Orange notified the registered Jews of the Sixth Order, recording in the Aliens Office file '*Each registered Jew verbally had his or her attention drawn to the Order*'.[20]

The Orders and measures imposed on the Jews had a substantial effect on the lives of those who remained in the islands. Some were subjected to closure of their businesses, deprived of the ability to obtain employment or earn a living in any way, curfew, repeated interviews, fear, deportation and ultimately death.

The First Order

'The (First) Order relating to Measures against the Jews' was registered in the Royal Courts of Guernsey on 23 October 1940 and Jersey on 21 October 1940 as Defence Regulation No 154 with the accompanying notices, Defence Regulation 156. The Order defined that '*those who belong or have belonged to the Jewish religion, or who have more than two Jewish grandparents, are deemed to be Jews. Grandparents who belong or have belonged to the Jewish religion are deemed to be Jews*'. American Jews were exempt from the Order. Jews were required to register at the Chief Aliens Office in Jersey, at the Office of the Inspector of Police in Guernsey and at the Seneschal in Sark. Declarants had to provide details of their surname, Christian name (sic), date of birth, place of birth, sex, family status, profession, religious faith and length of uninterrupted residence in the island. Jews who had '*fled from the occupied zone*' were forbidden to return. The Order in Jersey stated, '*The duty to register Jews has ... been delegated by the Bailiff ... to the Chief Aliens Officer*' and that *infractions of the Order were punishable by fine or imprisonment.'*

Clifford Orange, the Chief Aliens Officer placed a notice in the 'Jersey Evening Post', ordering all Jews to register at his office before 24

[19] C.W. Duret-Aubin CBE, 'Enemy Legislation and Judgements in Jersey' 1945; Casper, Remembrances, p.115; An original copy of this proclamation poster is in the collection of the Jersey Heritage Trust, Augres store.

[20] AO, Orders relating to measures against the Jews, GEN/3/1940.

October 1940. Twelve islanders made declarations to Clifford Orange and subsequently became categorised as *'registered Jews'* under the terms of the Order. Their names together with their dates of birth and nationalities were as follows:

Victor Emanuel 4/9/1870; British by naturalisation, born Germany; resident in Jersey for 2 years
John Finkelstein 12/3/1882; Romanian; resident in Jersey for 8 years
Samuel Selig Simon 3/6/1862; British, born in Jersey
Nathan Davidson 16/8/1881; Egyptian by naturalisation, born Romania; resident in Jersey for 5 years
Marianne Blampied 27/8/1887; British by marriage, born Holland; resident in Jersey for 2 years
John Jacobs 29/9/1883; British; resident in Jersey for 17 years
Theresa Marks 15/10/1862; born in Jersey
Ruby Ellen Still 4/7/1887; British; resident in Jersey for 30 years
Hyam Goldman 18/5/1869; British; resident in Jersey for 32 years
Hedwig Bercu 23/6/1919; Romanian, born Austria; resident in Jersey for 2 years
Margarete Hurban 16/4/1909; German, born Austria; resident in Jersey for 3 years
Esther Pauline Lloyd 31/7/1906; British; resident in Jersey for 3 years

Of this group Blampied, Davidson, Emanuel, Goldman, Hurban, Jacobs, Lloyd, and Still had Gentile spouses and they had not actively participated in maintaining Jewish community life in the island with the group previously listed as having left Jersey before the Occupation. Samuel Simon, however, although married to a Gentile, was a trustee of the Jewish cemetery at Westmount Road and he was from a long line of Jersey Jews who had arrived in the island in 1841. Theresa Marks was a member of the Leopold family, a long established Jersey Jewish family, and she had married Lewis Marks, also from a similar background. She was too ill to be evacuated and at the time of registration was living with her daughter Ruby Still; she died on 10 December 1940.[21] On 13

[21] Therese Leibman Marks(nee Leopold) and her husband Lewis who had died in 1916 were the last burials in the Jewish section of the Almorah cemetery, St Helier. Harry Leopold Marks became a trustee of the Westmount Jewish cemetery in 1924; in 1940 he evacuated from Jersey. Ruby Ellen Still married Albert Still, a Gentile in c.1925. Regal, 'History of the Jersey Jewish community'.

December she was buried in the Jewish section of Almorah cemetery in St Helier, however no headstone was placed to mark her grave.

John Finkelstein was a retired Egyptian government official who had been resident in the island for eight years but he had not associated with the island's pre-war Jewish community. Hedwig Bercu had arrived in the islands in November 1938 from Austria and was employed as in domestic service.

In Guernsey an order was placed in the *Guernsey Evening Press* on 24 October 1940 requiring Jews to report and register at the office of William Sculpher, the Inspector of Police. On 28 October 1940 Inspector Sculpher wrote to the Bailiff, Victor Carey stating that four Jews had registered in Guernsey, the Bailiff passed this information on the following day to KVR Dr Brosch at the Feldkommandantur.[22] The Bailiff subsequently sent on a report from Sark to Dr Brosch on 31 October listing one Jew, Annie Wranowsky, but adding that Wranowsky had stated that the 'J' on her German passport was a mistake. On the same day, Inspector Sclupher also prepared a report in relation to Julia Brichta, a Hungarian born 28 November 1895, who was then employed as a cook for the German authorities, specifying that this woman had stated that she was Protestant but that, '*further perusal of her passport will not reveal whether she is of pure Aryan birth - She was not asked the direct question*'. It is probable that the latter investigation was initiated by the Germans as a result of their analysis of the list of the religions of resident aliens that had been provided by Inspector Sculpher in August 1940.

A request was made for further information on Brichta and Wranowsky and on 7 November, Inspector Sculpher reported to Ambrose Sherwill, Guernsey Attorney-General, that both women had stated that they had no Jewish connections. This was passed on by John Leale, Acting President of the Controlling Committee, to the German authorities on the following day.

Annie Wranowsky was initially classified as a Jewess. Julia Brichta had arrived in the island in July 1939 and had been employed as a live-in domestic cook. On 10 September 1939 the Guernsey Police had visited her after she had gone on hunger strike complaining that her employers '*call me a spy and do not let me go out at all*'.[23] She was transferred to the Town Hospital and after recovery obtained new domestic employment. Her new employer decided to evacuate prior to the Occupation and wrote to the Inspector of Police stating that she had

[22] YV - Papers on Guernsey, Series 0.9.

[23] William Bell, I Beg to Report, (Guernsey, 1995), pp.25, 34.

given Julia Brichta five pounds and ordered her to report to the police station the following day.

In September 1940 Julia Brichta was implicated in the theft of a number of items from a hotel previously requisition by the German forces. She was not classified as a Jew and in April 1942 she married Jeremiah Barry, a non-Jew. In September 1943, however, she was denounced as a Jew and a black-marketeer to the German authorities. The first letter received by the Feldkommandantur on 16 September 1943 reads, '*Mrs Barry, a Hungarian Jew, just married for a business affair to escape your jurisdiction on Jews, carries on a very large bartering trade at her house'*.

An undated postcard was also received by the Feldkommandantur stating, '*We advise you to keep a watch on the Black Market activities of Mrs Barry*' and again a letter dated 30 September 1943, stated, '*She is truly a bad tongued Jew and an awful cheat'*. On 28 January 1944 Julia Brichta/Barry was sentenced on the orders of OKVR Dr. Casper of the Feldkommandantur to two weeks imprisonment and fined RM 200. She was again accused of black-marketeering and was deported on 5 May 1944 first to France and then to Ravensbrück concentration camp in Germany.[24]

She was one of thousands of women sanctioned for release on 21 April 1945. Brichta was handed over to the Red Cross and transferred to Sweden and after recovering her health she returned to Guernsey.

A report by Inspector Sculpher's of 25 November 1940 passed by the Bailiff to the German authorities summarised the names, dates of birth and nationalities of the registered Jews in Guernsey and Sark as follows:

> **Elda Brouard nee Bauer,** 27/4/1884, British by marriage, born Italy
> **Elisabet Duquemin nee Fink,** 21/7/1899, British by marriage, born Austria
> **Auguste Spitz,** 28/8/1901, German, born Austria
> **Therese Steiner,** 22/4/1916[25] German, born Austria
> **Anny (Annie) Wranowsky,** 22/4/1894, Czech but held German passport

Of the above, Brouard was a widow but had been married to a British subject in London; Duquemin was married to a non-Jewish Guernseyman; Spitz and Steiner were single and Wranowsky was a

[24] GAS, File FK 11-17; Bell, I Beg to Report, p.373: JEP letter 25 Feb 2000 confirmed that Julia Brichta was at Ravensbrück

[25] Therese Steiner's birth date is incorrectly stated, it was 24 Feb.1916.

divorcee. Brouard had arrived in the islands in August 1938; Duquemin in October 1937; Steiner in September 1939; Spitz in September 1937; and Wranowsky in August 1934.

The day after the promulgation of the First Order, Jersey's Royal Court registered Defence Regulation 157, defining Jewish businesses as such '*if an interest therein exceeding 50% is owned by Jews'*. The businesses were ordered to carry the notice '*JUDISCHES GESCHAFT - Jewish Undertaking*'. The order required that '*the marking of Jewish businesses, particularly shops, hotels, etc must be carried out by means of a printed notice to be affixed to the inner side of all shop windows. The notices are to be 20cm by 40cm in size and yellow in colour'*. Declarations in Jersey were to be made direct to the Attorney-General.

The Attorney-General on the Bailiff's instructions placed a notice of the Order in the 'Jersey Evening Post' and three business declarations were made direct to him in response. On 26 October 1940 the manager of Montague Burton's branch declared to the Attorney-General '*I am unable to state if any or what capital is held by persons of Jewish origin*'. The following day the manager of Jays Furnishings declared '*I beg to state that, to the best of my knowledge and belief, one of the Directors of the Company is of Jewish origin....but I am quite unable to give any information as to the percentage of shares in the Company which may be held by Jews*'. On 29 October Advocate De la Haye made a declaration on behalf of his client Mrs Sweeney, who was administrator for Mark and Ethel Green who prior to their evacuation ran a ladies clothes shop 'Madame Eve' in St Helier. De la Haye declared, '*There appears to be some doubt as to whether or not the said Mr Green was either a Jew or of Jewish extraction*' and enclosed a declaration signed by Mrs Sweeney stating that Mrs Green had been '*a regular attendant at St Helier's Parish Church*'. The Attorney-General forwarded the three declarations to the Bailiff for onward transmission to the Feldkommandant for a decision. The Feldkommandant determined that the three businesses would not be required to display a 'Jewish Undertakings' sign.

The Second Order

'The Second Order relating to Measures against the Jews' was registered in the Royal Courts of Guernsey on 27 November 1940 and Jersey on 16 November 1940 as Defence Regulation No 174. This ordered:

> *'All Jewish economic undertakings, all Jews, all husbands and wives of Jews, and all bodies corporate which are not economic undertakings but more than one third of whose members or*

> *managers are Jews shall ... declare to the Bailiff ... the shares belonging ... to them, their beneficial interest in the business, their sleeping interest in economic undertakings and loans to such undertakings, their real estate and interest therein.'*

All legal transactions entered into after 23 May 1940 relating to the sale of goods by Jews were declared null and void. Administrators were authorised to be named for Jewish businesses and penalties for infractions included imprisonment, fine and confiscation.

The Second Order carried an attached notice signed by Clifford Orange requiring under the '*the power vested [in him] ... by the Bailiff ... that undertakings, persons and bodies specified in ..... the said Order must send or deliver the required declarations to the Aliens Office.*'

On 22 November Orange informed administrators that even if they were in doubt as to whether a client was a Jew or not they must make a declaration. Orange interviewed at least two firms of administrators advising them that '*the sole responsibility for failing to make declaration of the property of Jews would lie on the Administrators of persons absent from the island, who may possibly be Jews, but in regard to whom the legal Administrators are in doubt'*. This interview led to the declaration made by Bois & Bois in respect of Mr and Mrs Dudley and Mr and Mrs Marks although their administrator in defence of his client made it clear that '*it is impossible to definitely state that they are in fact Jews*'.[26]

This Second Order resulted in two declarations being made by resident Jews and a further nine by the legal administrators of Jews who had left Jersey prior to the Occupation. The correspondence relating to these declarations makes up nearly half of Clifford Orange's Aliens Office file 'Orders relating to Measures against the Jews'.

On 27 Nov. 1940 Clifford Orange provided a summary to the Bailiff of these declarations as follows: Mr Harry Leopold Marks; Commercial Properties Ltd; Mr Phineas Cohen; Mr Alfred Krichefski; Mr Nathan Davidson; Mr Hyam Goldman; Mr and Mrs Simon Peretz; Mr Israel Cohen; Mr and Mrs Dudley Marks; Mr Louis Feldman; Mr and Mrs Beryl Bernard Silver.[27]

---

[26] JAS File GEN/3/1940, Letter from Bois and Bois to C. Orange 25 Nov 1940

[27] Beryl and Blanche Silver were the parents of Esther Lloyd. After the war the Silvers moved to Israel. Beryl Silver bequeathed part of his remaining property in Jersey, the site of his old summer house at St Ouen, to the State of Israel.

The *Aryanization* of Jewish businesses

On 11 December 1940 the Feldkommandant wrote to the Bailiff of Jersey requiring that he be provided within seven days with a full list of businesses marked under the terms of the First Order as 'Jewish Undertakings'. The Germans also required details of the turnover and stock of each business and the name of the administrators. The matter was delegated to Clifford Orange in consultation with the Attorney-General. On 14 December Orange placed a notice in the 'Jersey Evening Post' requiring declarations in respect of 'Jewish Undertakings' detailing the name of the proprietor, the nature of the business, a list of branches or side-lines, turnover and value of stock. On 18 December Orange provided copies of the resultant declarations to the Bailiff as follows:

> Mr Nathan Davidson, Groceries fruit and vegetable store, 38 Stopford Road, St Helier; Sidelines newspapers; Turnover £250; Stock £10.
>
> Mrs Hyam Goldman, Grocery and General Store, St Peter's Valley; Stock £10.17s.6d.
>
> Louis et Cie (Mr Louis Feldman), 5 New Street, St Helier; Administrator Advocate J F Le Cornu; Costumier and Milliner; Turnover £3,978; Stock £200; Cash £325; Other Investments £800 3 ½% War Loan and 1,000 Shares in Morris Motors Ltd.
>
> Messrs A Krichefski and Son, 18 Hilgrove Street, St Helier; Administrator Le Masurier Giffard and Poch; Men's outfitter; Turnover £6392; Stock £1800.
>
> Madame Peretz, 9 King Street, St Helier; Administrator Le Masurier Giffard and Poch; Costumier and Milliner; Turnover £2,940; Stock £100.

The Feldkommandant again wrote to the Bailiff on 30 December requiring that a new notice '*Under the administration of an Aryan Administrator in virtue of the Order of 18 October 1940*' must be displayed in German and English on Jewish undertakings. In this letter the Feldkommandant noted that administrators had been appointed for Louis et Cie, Krichefski and Son and Madame Peretz but not for Nathan Davidson's or Hyam Goldman's businesses. The Feldkommandant asked the Bailiff to recommend a suitable administrator for these small concerns and instructed that as soon as he had approved the appointment of a recommended administrator the two businesses should display the new sign. The Feldkommandant also asked the Bailiff, '*to examine the question as to whether a closing or sale to an Aryan is possible. The complicated procedure of appointing an administrator would then be obviated*'.

Hyam Goldman had first declared his business to Clifford Orange by letter on 22 November 1940, stating:

> '*I beg to declare I have a small grocer shop (Bee Hive Stores) ... a J.U. [Jewish Undertaking] poster is on the window. Not*

> *withstanding the above, by Jersey Judicatory (sic), the above is 5% Jewish 95 non Jewish this condition having been stable since 1908.'*

Nathan Davidson on 23 November made the following declaration to Orange:

> *'I am not sure whether I come under the province of the above order, but in case I do. I declare the following: I am running a small grocery shop which I am winding up at present and beyond a small banking account I have no other assets or property whatever.'*

Clifford Orange instructed Hyam Goldman and Nathan Davidson to attend at the Office of the Attorney-General on 2 January 1941. On 3 January the Attorney-General wrote to the Bailiff stating that he had interviewed Mrs Goldman and Mr Davidson, and had given them the option of either appointing administrators or closing their businesses, he stated both had decided to close their businesses. On 10 January the Bailiff replied that the Feldkommandant had ordered that their business must be closed before 25 January. On the following day the Attorney-General instructed both to close their businesses and to report to him in writing '*when the winding up of your business is actually completed*'.

On 23 January Nathan Davidson wrote to the Attorney-General:

> *'In accordance with your instructions I beg to inform you that I have finished the winding up of my business...the blind on the window pulled down and a notice CLOSED displayed'.*

Davidson, having lost his business premises, was forced to move to new accommodation at 59 Oxford Road, St Helier later that day.[28]

Mrs Goldman having received the Attorney-General's instructions to close Beehive Stores attended the Feldkommandant's office to protest that the business belonged to her and not her husband. She protested that as she was not a Jew the business therefore should not be regarded as a Jewish Undertaking. The Feldkommandant immediately ordered the Attorney-General '*to examine the matter*' as it '*would not, in my opinion, be considered a Jewish undertaking*'.

On 18 January the Attorney-General wrote to Mrs Goldman requiring her to attend an interview: *'It is desirable that you should bring your legal adviser with you as it will be necessary for him...to certify the accuracy of all the facts set out in the statement of your case as submitted by you to the Field Command.'*

---

[28] Davidson's Registration Card confirms his move to 59 Oxford Road on 23 January 1941

Accordingly on 21 January Mrs Goldman and Advocate Bois attended the Attorney-General's office, after which Aubin wrote to the Bailiff stating that he believed Mrs Goldman's statements to be true and enclosed an affidavit he had required her to swear confirming that she, as the owner of the shop, was not a Jew.

On 24 January the Feldkommandant informed the Bailiff that *'It has been established that Mrs Goldman...is not a Jewess in terms of .... the Order concerning Jews dated 27th September 1940....Mrs Goldman's shop can therefore, in future, be considered as a non-Jewish undertaking. The mark is to be removed.'*

Having ensured that registered Jews were not operating business, the Germans turned their attention to the *Aryanization* of Jewish businesses under administration. On 21 November 1940 Advocate J. Le Cornu, of Ogier and Le Cornu, had written to Clifford Orange as administrator for Mr Louis Feldman who *was 'the sole owner of an undertaking in furs and gowns at No 5 New Street. The business is managed by Miss Hawkins, a British subject'*. On 22 November Orange had replied to Le Cornu stating that he must declare any further business interests belonging to Louis Feldman including rents and mortgages receivable, shares in any undertaking in Jersey or any other German occupied territory and interest derivable from Mr Feldman's real estate. Clifford Orange annotated this letter: *'No written reply received. Advocate Le Cornu informed me by telephone, when I pointed out to him that I had not received a reply, that he had nothing to add to his written statement of the 21 November 1940'*.

Four months later, on 18 March 1941, in response to the Feldkommandant's instructions to the Bailiff, Jersey's Attorney-General wrote to Advocate Le Cornu stating that *'In accordance with a recent Order of the District Chief in St Germain, measures are to be taken whereby Jewish Undertakings are to be sold as quickly as possible to Aryans. The transactions with regard to the sales are to be carried out by the temporary administrator. The contract is to be submitted to the Field Command before being concluded'*. He added that sales at an under-valuation were not permissible and advertisements were to be placed in the Jersey and Guernsey newspapers. The Feldkommandantur wished to be informed of the progress of the sales before 25 March 1941. Copies of this letter were sent to Le Masurier and Giffard and Poch as administrators for Messrs Krichefski and Son and 'Madame Peretz'.

The administrators placed advertisements in the 'Jersey Evening Post' offering, *'for sale by tender, the undertaking, including the stock-in-trade'* of Louis et Cie, Madame Peretz and A. Krichefski.[29]

On 25 March, Advocate Le Cornu notified the Attorney-General that he had only received one tender for Mr Feldman's business, being an offer of £150 from the manageress, Miss Hawkins. Advocate Le Cornu noted that, *'A list has been made of the Stock and by reason of information I have received from an independent source the sum of £150 offer by Miss Hawkins seems fair and reasonable'*. However the papers in the possession of the Feldman family reveal that Advocate Le Cornu had also received one opportunist letter from a costumier in Guernsey seeking to purchase items of stock only.

The Attorney-General wrote to Advocate Le Cornu on 15 April 1941 stating, *'Field Command 515 ... had no objection to the conclusion of a contract on the basis stated in your said letter.'* On 21 April the agreement for sale was submitted, via the Attorney-General, to the Feldkommandantur for approval. On 30 April Advocate Le Cornu informed the Attorney-General that the sale to Miss Hawkins had been 'concluded this morning'.

Administrators Le Masurier Giffard & Poch acting for both A. Krichefski & Son and Madam Peretz also only received offers from the shops' managers. Mr John Beaton offered £1,050 for Krichefski's business and Miss White offered £50 for Madame Peretz. On 10 April the Feldkommandant informed the Bailiff that he could *'only agree to these sales if the suitability of the tenders is certified by an expert'*. The expert opinion was provided by Noel and Porter (removers and warehousemen) and on 2 June the Feldkommandant authorised the sales.

The progress of the local *Aryanization* program was of monitored by the German commanders in France. On 24 June the Feldkommandant wrote to the Bailiff noting *'The Military Commander in France will shortly be asking for a report concerning the position with regard to all cases of Aryanization. I request therefore that you will speedily conclude the sales'*. The two remaining draft contacts of sale were submitted to the Attorney-General by Le Masurier Giffard & Poch as administrators on 28 June and the Feldkommandant informed the Bailiff on 4 July that the contacts were acceptable. Le Masurier Giffard & Poch wrote to the Attorney-General on 10 July noting: *'The matters are being completed forthwith.'*

---

[29] Jersey Evening Post, 19-23 March 1941

In another arm of the *Aryanization* program and possibly due to monitoring by his superiors in France , the Feldkommandant ordered the sale of shares held by Alfred and Wilfred Harold Krichefski in local companies. The Attorney-General instructed that the shares be offered for tender in the local press. An advertisement was placed in the 'Jersey Evening Post' on 2 July and Le Masurier Giffard & Poch reported to

Attorney-General the highest tenders he had received:

> From Mr C. Le Gallais the sum of 16/- per share for 40 shares in Jersey Recreation Grounds and 5/- per share for 50 shares in J Bigwood Ltd
>
> From Mrs E. Le C. Pearce the sum of 21/- per share for 425 shares in West Pictures (Jersey) Ltd.

On 11 August the Attorney-General informed the administrators that the sale of the shares had been approved by the Feldkommandant.

It would appear that the sales of the businesses belonging to the Krichefski, Peretz and Feldman families were constructed transactions intended to protect the assets of the absent Jews, arranged between their administrators and the managers. Two letters provide evidence of the straw-man nature of the sales. In 1945 after liberation Jack Beaton wrote to Wilfred Krichefski (on hearing of the death of his father Alfred) noting: *'I had always, during the bad times, thought "one day this will all be over and I shall feel Mr Alfred's hand on my shoulder and hear his voice saying 'Well done, Jack'"*. Immediately after the Liberation, Advocate Le Cornu wrote to Louis Feldman noting *'Miss Hawkins ... has worked splendidly; you owe her a deep debt of gratitude ... all Jewish businesses had to be sold and the proceeds of sale frozen. This was done with the help of Miss Hawkins, and generally speaking all your interests have been preserved. I have a deposit of £540 waiting for you at the Jersey Savings bank.'*

One puzzling area is just how the managers were able to pay for the businesses, as the contacts of sale noted that the administrators received the sales proceeds on the execution of the contacts. Just how Mr Beaton, Miss Hawkins, and Miss White were able to find £1050, £150, and £50 respectively is not clear. There is no indication that the businesses were sold at anything less than their true wartime value but the contracts themselves transferred the minimum of assets and the contracts were certainly unusual effectively just covering the sale of stock. No attempt was made to transfer the freehold of the properties and no mention was made in the sale contracts of any post-sale rental due. The deficiencies of the contracts reinforce the straw-man aspect of the transactions but exactly how much of the sham nature of the sales was known to the Crown Officers is unclear.

The matter of the consideration monies is further complicated by the terms of the Fifth Order against the Jews. This required that administrators should deposit the proceeds of the sales of the *Aryanization* program with the States of Jersey's Department of Finance and Economics. On 15 November 1941 The Attorney-General wrote to Le Masurier, Giffard and Poch and Advocate Le Cornu *'to request you to deal in accordance with that Order with any funds in your hands which may be affected thereby'*. Le Masurier Giffard and Poch replied: *'The matter is receiving our attention'*. On 21 November Advocate Le Cornu replied *'I have now complied with the Order'*. The Attorney-general's file contains no further references to this matter and it is unclear if any funds were ever handed over to the States department.

In 1946 Louis Feldman made a claim for compensation for his wartime losses to the States of Jersey, Channel Islands (Property) Rehabilitation Scheme, War Damage committee. However this claim did not specifically address the fact that much of his loss had been directly attributable to the *Aryanization* of Jewish business program and his claim was processed in the same way as other damage and confiscation claims. Although Advocate Le Cornu provided Louis Feldman with some of the wartime correspondence relating to the *Aryanization* program, he did pass on a copy of the sale contract and Feldman was not made aware of the exact process of *Aryanization*. Consequently no claim was ever made specifically in relation to the confiscation of Jewish business assets.

It seems that after the war the Krichefski and Peretz business assets were also handed back largely in tact after the Occupation. Curiously Clifford Orange prevented the Peretz family from obtaining immediate access to their business although after a few days access was granted. In a letter sent to the Attorney-General on 1 August 1945 Dudley Marks also provides an indication that Clifford Orange was indifferent to his efforts to reclaim his business assets. Marks wrote *'My solicitors Bois & Bois and Lloyds Bank have repeatedly asked me to come across as they need me badly.....I don't think Mr Orange as [sic] anything against me, I am informed by Mr Le Gresley .. that he wrote Mr Orange and got no reply'*. Due to the restrictions on the issue of travel permits at the time the Solicitor General acting on behalf of the Attorney-general did not grant a permit to Marks.[30]

[30] Author's interview with Eve Peretz; JAS Law Officers Files D/Z

The property and investment interests of Israel and Phineas Cohen were substantially handed back by their administrators after Liberation.[31]

Declarations under the First and Second Orders had also been made in relation to Jewish business interests in Guernsey. A letter from Inspector Sculpher to the Bailiff dated 23 October 1940 stated that the managers of Messrs Hipps Ltd and Montague Burton Ltd were *'unable to say whether over 50% of the Firm's Capital is in Jewish hands'*. Sculpher advised them that they need not display a 'Jewish Undertaking' sign.[32]

On 2 December 1040 Violet Bland Woolnough made a declaration to the Greffier listing her investments and stating: *'my mother (now deceased) was a Jewess, but my father is a Gentile'*. Mr W. Falla declared that he was renting premises *'from Mr David Rudnidsky, whom I believe is a Jew, and when last heard of was residing at ... Winchester Road, Andover, Hants, England'*.

The Deputy Custodian of Unoccupied Dwellings and the Custodian of Business and Industry both wrote on 3 December to the Greffier of Guernsey's Royal Court in relation to the ladies retail business operated by Mr and Mrs W. Middlewick, who had evacuated prior to the Occupation. The Bailiff subsequently instructed the Custodian of Business and Industry to sell the goods left in the island by the Middlewicks and on 3 May 1941 the Custodian confirmed to the Bailiff that his order had been carried out.

After the war the Middlewicks made a successful application to the Channel Islands (Property) Rehabilitation Scheme for compensation for their loss of business equipment, stock in trade and personal chattels. The compensation payments included the sum of £221-17-0 from the Custodian of Businesses. Similarly David Rudnidsky made a successful application relating to damage to his property during the Occupation.[33]

In Jersey, Clifford Orange and Mr Le Couteur, the acting Royal Court Greffier examined the Register of Contracts, the Register of Loans and the Register of Limited Liability Companies in connection with the requirements of the Second Order. On 30 November 1940 Orange reported to the Bailiff that John Jacobs one of the registered Jews had sold No. 4 St Clements Gardens for £800 in June 1940. Orange also

[31] Author's interview with Mrs R. Senett, June 1997. Israel Cohen's properties at Georgetown, St Helier were not sold by his administrator. The assets of Phineas Cohen primarily comprised stocks and bonds in companies outside the Islands (and occupied Europe) and whilst substantial, could not practically have been sold or transferred by his administrator. Much of the family's moveable assets situate in their properties - furniture, household goods, etc. - were lost during the Occupation.

[32] YV, Papers on Guernsey Series 0.9.

[33] GAS Rehabilitation files

reported that Dudley Marks's administrator had incurred a loan on his client's behalf of £1,000 in August 1940.[34] Orange however reported that he was unable to complete his enquiries as the Register of Limited Liability Companies would not be completed until January 1941. On 3 January 1941 the Feldkommandant instructed the Bailiff to make a full return of Jewish transactions as soon as the register was closed.

Clifford Orange's subsequent analysis of the Register of Limited Liability Companies show that he went to extraordinary lengths to identify islanders of possible Jewish origin who had not declared themselves as Jews. His hand written notes of February 1941 show that he had identified three individuals of possible Jewish descent; William Leopold, Alfred Ephraums and Ferdinand Lowenstein. Orange noted: *'There is a William Henry Leopold of Corner House, St Brelade who holds 200 Ord. and 250 Pref. shares in Bon Air Nursing Home, but he has not registered as a Jew'*. William Leopold was known by islanders to be a Jew and remained undetected throughout the Occupation.[35] Orange also noted: *'Jersey New Waterworks Company - Jersey Electric Company - Alfred Francis Ephraums - Leyton, Green Street, St Helier'* and *'Ferdinand Marcus Lowenstein, 90 St Saviours Road - 7 - £1 shares in Jersey Recreation Grounds Company - qy (sic) of Jewish descent'*. Alfred Ephraums remained in the islands throughout the Occupation.[36] It is probable that Lowenstein had died before the war.[37]

Whatever the reasons for his search for persons of Jewish descent who may have had entries in the Register, Orange did not pass their names. On 11 February 1941 having completed the investigation Clifford Orange and the Judicial Greffier, Mr A Le Riche wrote to the Bailiff noting *'With regard to the names of shareholders contained in the*

---

[34] Kelly's Channel Islands Directory of 1939 lists Violet B. Woolnough ALCM LLCB as a 'teacher of music' at Vauvert Manor, St Peter Port, Guernsey; Island of Jersey, AO, Orders relating to measures against Jews, GEN/3/1940.

[35] JAS, Registration card. Mr R. Le Sueur wrote to the author in July 1997 and stated that his father was a friend of 'Willy Leopold' and that although he was always known to be Jewish he was never detected by the German authorities. William Leopold's identity card notes that he was born on 24 January 1880 in St Helier and lists his address at that time as Parade Road, St Helier. He is recorded as married and employed as a grocer's manager. Leopold was a cousin of Theresa Marks who was a registered Jew. The Leopold family were a well-established Jersey Jewish family. Leopold's great uncle had been the President of the Jersey Jewish Congregation until his death in 1877.

[36] Alfred Ephraums registered under the 'Registration and Identification of Persons Order' in January 1941. He was born on 22 December 1884 in Ceylon and is listed as married and without an occupation - probably retired. Alfred Francis Ephraums obtained a new passport in 1938, Gladys Isabel Ephraums and Walter Francis Ephraums obtained new passports in September 1939.

[37] A Ferdinand Marcus Lowenstein is buried at the Westmount Jewish cemetery. His father, of the same name is buried adjacent.

Register, we have established that the shares held by persons definitely known to be Jews have already been declared in accordance with the requirement of the Order'.

The Third Order

'The Third Order', registered in the Royal Courts of Guernsey on 17 June 1941 and of Jersey on 31 May 1941 as Regulation and Order No 307, redefined those persons considered to be Jewish:

> *Any person having at least three grandparents of pure Jewish blood shall be deemed to be a Jew. A grandparent having belonged to the Jewish religious community shall be deemed to be of pure Jewish blood.*
>
> *Any person having two grandparents of pure Jewish blood who:*
>
> *(a)... belongs to the Jewish religious community or who subsequently joins it; or*
>
> *(b) ... is married to a Jew or subsequently marries a Jew; shall be deemed to be a Jew.*
>
> *In doubtful cases any person who belongs or has belonged to the Jewish religious community shall be deemed to be a Jew.*

The order prohibited Jews and Jewish owned businesses, not in the hands of an administrator, from carrying out many economic activities including, wholesale and retail, hotel and catering, insurance, navigation, dispatch and storage, guides, banking and money exchange, and businesses concerned with dealings in apartments, land and mortgages. Further, no Jew was to be engaged as a *'higher official or as an employee who comes into contact with customers'* and Jewish employees should *'be dismissed and replaced by non-Jewish employees'*. Managing administrators, authorised to sell holdings and shares, could be appointed to administer holdings in limited liability companies and shares belonging to Jews and Jewish undertakings. No compensation was to be paid for losses incurred by Jews as a result of carrying out the order and no compensation was to be paid for dismissing a Jewish employee without notice. Infractions were punishable by fine and imprisonment *'unless a more severe penalty is otherwise prescribed'*.

On 8 June 1941 the Feldkommandant wrote to Bailiff Coutanche asking for confirmation that no Jews were carrying on businesses prohibited under the Third Order. On 13 June, Clifford Orange was able to inform the Bailiff that *'there are no Jews, registered as such, in the island who are carrying on businesses'*[38]

The Third Order resulted in Ada Isaacs and Agnes Delikat visiting the Aliens Office to enquire as to whether they should make declarations under the revised definition of who was considered to be a Jew under the Order as they had Jewish connections. In both cases Clifford Orange advised them to write to him so that he could pass on their letters to the Germans for a decision. Agnes Delikat was known to Orange as she had made a declaration to him under the Second Order but Orange had marked her letter *'nothing declarable'*

On 3 June 1941 a Mr Saunders attended the Aliens Office and Orange made the following file note:

> *Mr Saunders, Manager of the Ommaroo Hotel, called to see me and asked whether Moss Simon, employed by him as a hotel porter, was affected by the Order. Simon is not registered as a Jew as it appears, according to Mr Saunders information, that Simon's paternal grandparents only were Jews, his mother being a Gentile. I advised Mr Saunders to tell Simon to write to me on the matter, giving all particulars, and said I would forward his letter when received to the competent authorities for a decision. Mr Saunders said that this would be done.*[39]

Moss Simon stated, in his declaration to Orange curiously dated the day before Saunders' visit to the Aliens Office, that his father was a Jew (Samuel Selig Simon) but that his mother was a Gentile.

On 20 June 1941 the Feldkommandant advised the Bailiff that Simon, Isaacs and Delikat were not to be regarded as Jewish. However, perhaps in consequence of the report the Feldkommandant was required to make to his superiors in France, the issue of Delikat, Simon and Isaacs was raised again. On 4 July the Feldkommandant ordered that further investigations were to be carried out.

On 11 July, having ordered each to attend an interview, Orange notified the Bailiff that only Moss Simon had any Jewish connections but that even he had a Gentile mother. Finally, on 12 August the Feldkommandant informed the Bailiff that all three had been classified as not Jewish.

Both the Aliens Office and Law Officers files contain correspondence detailing the investigations undertaken by Clifford Orange in relation to Catherine Hill, nee Jacobs. Hill's legal representatives, Le Masurier

---

[38] Island of Jersey, AO, Orders relating to measures against Jews, GEN/3/1940;.

[39] Island of Jersey, AO, Orders relating to measures against Jews, GEN/3/1940.

Giffard and Poch, had submitted her name in a letter of 23 November 1940 to the Aliens Office listing three clients who had left the island prior to the Occupation and *'all bear names which we believe are of Jewish origin'*. Hence, on 3 January 1941 the Feldkommandant wrote to the Bailiff requiring declarations of assets in respect of Catherine Pauline Hill, Sydney Bernard Podro and Jack Morris Israel.

Clifford Orange requested further information and 13 January Le Masurier Giffard and Poch listed the assets of their three clients, but noted, *'we have no further evidence to establish that Mrs Hill is in fact a Jewess'*. Five months later the Feldkommandantur again raised the issue of Hill, advising the Bailiff on 8 June 1941, *'would you kindly inform me what facts have given rise for the supposition that Mrs Catherine Pauline Hill, nee Jacobs, is a Jewess'*. On 11 June Clifford Orange wrote to Le Masurier Giffard and Poch for clarification and they replied stating that apart from the fact her maiden name was Jacobs which *'may be of Jewish origin'* there was no other reason to assume that she was Jewish.

On 20 June the Feldkommandant wrote to the Bailiff noting that *'the name Jacobs cannot be regarded as only being Jewish. It strikes me however that in the enclosure accompanying your letter of 17 March 1941 – W 30/17 a John Jacobs is listed as being Jewish. Is he related to Mrs Hill?'* Clifford Orange, given the task of determining the relationship between Catherine Hill and John Jacobs called him in for interview on 24 June. In the Aliens Office Registration diary only Mrs Jacobs is listed as attending, John Jacobs is noted as being too ill to attend. On the same day Clifford Orange wrote to the Bailiff confirming that Mrs Hill and John Jacobs were distantly related. On 4 July 1941 the Feldkommandant's office wrote to the Bailiff stating:

> *'In view of the relationship between Mr John Jacobs and Mrs Hill it must now be taken that Mrs Hill is a Jewess. Messrs. Le Masurier, Giffard and Poch must therefore sell the shares and bonds of the Jersey Gas Light Company, the Jersey New Waterworks Company, the Jersey Electricity Company and Messrs C. J. Dupre – Kindly inform me of the action taken.'*

From this time the matter of Mrs Hill was largely dealt with by the Attorney-General rather than Orange.

The following day the Attorney-General informed Advocate Poch that the Feldkommandant had directed that *'Mrs Hill is to be considered a Jewess'* and that her shares and bonds were to be sold. The Attorney-General requested to be notified when the sales were completed.

On 16 July Catherine Hill's administrator Mr Poch called to see Clifford Orange advising that he wished to appeal against the decision that his client be deemed a Jew.

On 25 July Advocate Poch wrote to the Attorney-General pointing out:

> *'Since we first wrote to the Chief Aliens Officer intimating to him that certain of our clients bore names which we believe were of Jewish origin, we have ascertained that there is another resident of Jersey whose surname is Jacobs... This gentleman claims that there is a distant degree of relationship between himself and Mrs Hill, but he informed us that Mrs Hill denied any relationship. Mr John Jacobs informs us that, although he made declaration that he was a Jew, neither he nor his brothers have followed the Jewish faith. Mr Jacobs knows nothing of the Jewish religion; he has married an Aryan and his children were baptized in the Anglican Church.'*

Poch concluded by appealing to the Attorney-General: *'if you would kindly ask the Field Commandant graciously to re-consider his directions in order that Mrs Hill's small holdings in local companies be not sold. Mrs Hill is advancing in years and any diminution in her income would be a serious hardship.'*

On 12 August the Feldkommandant wrote to the Bailiff *'I request that you ascertain if the relationship can be proved authentically (entries such as church registers etc). The sale of the shares is postponed until the position is finally clarified.'* On 19 August Advocate Poch notified the Attorney-General that John Jacobs could not provide any *'documentary evidence'* and that *'Mrs Hill denied any relationship to him.'* On 29 August the Attorney-General notified Advocate Poch that Mrs Hill's shares need not be sold. [40] Advocate Poch's principled appeal had succeeded.

The Feldkommandantur advised the Controlling Committee of the States of Guernsey to instigate further enquiries into the financial circumstances of the registered Jews resident in the island.[41] On 14 January 1942 Inspector Sculpher submitted a report detailing the assets of Elisabeth Duquemin and Elda Brouard. Duquemin, he declared, had *'no income, she owns no property, has no investments. She has £83 in the Post office Savings bank, this money is being saved for the education*

[40] JAS File DZ 'Jewish Undertakings etc'; The registrar of the Jersey Electricity Company has confirmed to the author that the £300 3 1/2% Debenture that Mrs Hill held in the company and declared to Clifford Orange by her administrators on 13 Jan. 1941 was not sold by her administrators during the Occupation.

[41] YV, Papers on Guernsey Series 0.9.

of her child'. Elda Brouard, he declared, *'is ... employed as a housekeeper earning 10/- cash and her board and lodgings each week. She owns no property. She has £250 invested in War Loan and £80 deposited in Barclay's bank'*. The President of the Controlling Committee was to obtain the necessary financial information relating to Steiner and Spitz from the Secretary of the Castel Hospital. On the following day the President of the Controlling Committee passed on Sculpher's report together with a covering letter declaring, that Steiner *'is a nurse with a salary of £48.10.0 per annum and board and lodging and Miss Spitz is a housemaid earning 15/- per week and board and lodging. Neither of them has any other assets'*.

On 14 January 1942 the Assistant Aliens Officer in Jersey was required to attend at the Feldkommandantur with a list of Jews resident in the island together with their property and business interests.

The most extensive entry relating to Jews in the Aliens Office Registration diary relates to this enquiry. It was written by the Assistant Registration Officer and is the only diary entry not in the hand of Clifford Orange:

> *Thursday 13 January 1942*
>
> *4.15pm Field Command, College House, Room 15, telephoned inquiring if any Jews whose names appeared on the lists submitted to them on 15 March 1941, have died or left the island. I informed him that to the best of my knowledge all the persons on the list are still alive and on the island.*
>
> *4.30pm Second telephone call from College House Room 15, asking for a list of all properties, shares etc owned by Jews. I informed him that the files were locked away and that Mr Orange had the keys, and was at home ill. I promised to communicate with him tomorrow morning.*
>
> *Wednesday 14 January 1942*
>
> *10:15am Telephoned to College House, to inquire if the lists asked for of properties etc. belonging to Jews, included those who had evacuated previous to the occupation, or only those still resident here. He promised to inform me later.*
>
> *11:30am College House, Room 15 telephoned and informed me that a list of persons and their properties now on the island was only required at present. But they would like to see our file concerning Jews out of the island, and would consider what other information was required.*

> *4.00pm I attended at College House, Room 15, with a list and file of the Jews. After consultation he decided that we should also submit a list of all the Jews out of the island and their administration. I was also requested to inform the following persons to attend at College House, Room 15, tomorrow, Thursday: - Mrs M. Blampied (nee Van Abbe), Mr Victor Emanuel, Mr Samuel Selig Simon & Miss Hedy Bercu.*[42]

On 16 January, the Assistant Registration Officer wrote to the Feldkommandantur enclosing a list of Jews who had evacuated before the Occupation but included the caveat *'that it had not been definitely established that all the persons mentioned in the enclosed list are Jews'.*[43] The assistant Registration Officer added that that he had ordered Blampied, Emanuel, Simon and Bercu to attend at College House, however the purpose of the interviews is not evident from the surviving correspondence.

An entry in the Aliens Office diary of 16 January 1942, again in the Assistant Registration Officers hand, notes *'11.00 am Miss Hedy Bercu called and informed me that she had not yet called at College House. I cautioned her, and told her to proceed there as soon as possible'.*[44]

The Fourth, Fifth and Sixth Orders

'The Fourth Order' was not Registered on an instruction of the Feldkommandantur dated 10 June 1941, as it only related to one Jewish company in Jersey, Commercial Properties Ltd, who were informed of the content.[45]

'The Fifth Order relating to measures against Jews' and accompanying Notice were registered in the Royal Courts of Guernsey on 28 October 1941 and of Jersey on 1 November 1941, as Regulation and Order No 422 and No 423. The Order stated that administrators of Jewish undertakings should, on the termination of their management, deposit the net proceeds with the Jersey Department of Finance and Economics.

As stated above Le Masurier Giffard and Poch and Advocate Le Cornu as administrators of *Aryanised* Jewish businesses were notified of the

[42] JID, AO Diary - Registration and Identification of persons (Jersey) Order 1940, 6 Jan. 1941 - 10 Oct. 1942.

[43] AO file – Orders relating to measures against the Jews GEN/3/1940 -List of evacuated Jews dated 14 January 1942

[44] AO file – Orders relating to measures against the Jews GEN/3/1940; AO diary – Registration and Identification of persons Order 1940.

[45] JAS, file, Aliens Office, Island of Jersey - Orders relating to measures against Jews, GEN/3/1940. Letter signed by Dr Gottfried von Stein

terms of the Order. Le Masurier Giffard and Poch notified the Attorney-General that *'the matter is receiving our attention'* and Advocate Le Cornu declared to the Attorney General, *'I have now complied with the Order'*. Exactly how much was handed over is unclear, however the program for the *Aryanization* of Jewish businesses in Jersey and Guernsey was now complete.

'The Sixth Order' was registered in Guernsey on 21 March 1942 and Jersey on 7 March 1942 as Regulation and Order No 519. The Order established a curfew from 8.00pm until 6.00am for Jews. Furthermore Jews were no longer permitted to change their place of residence without consent. This order, in addition to fine and imprisonment, for the first time listed as a penalty for non-compliance that *'the offender may be interned in a camp for Jews'*.

The Aliens Office file contains notes of the change of residence of Hedwig Bercu, Margarete Hurban, Samuel Simon and Marianne Blampied under the terms of this Order.[46]

On 6 Feb. 1942 KVR Dr Reffler of the Feldkommandant telexed the Nebenstelle in Guernsey requiring immediate information as to whether any of the residences of the registered Jews in Guernsey had been requisitioned by the German authorities, adding that the Guernsey civilian officers were not to deal with this matter. The reply, dated the following day, listing the addresses of the four registered Jews in the island also noted that up to that time no Jewish residences had been requisitioned in Guernsey.

It would seem therefore that as in many other Occupied areas, the possibility of confiscating the homes of registered Jews was considered but unusually this was not taken further in the Channel Islands. Theresa Steiner and Auguste Spitz remained in accommodation at the Country Hospital, Castel and were in any case deported ultimately to Auschwitz-Birkenau two months later. Elda Brouard and Elisabet Duquemin remained at their pre-war places of residence until their deportation in February 1943. Furthermore the Feldkommandantur do not appear to have followed the policy adopted in other occupied areas of confiscating and selling of the personal chattels of registered Jews. On 29 April 1942 KVR Dr Reffler notified the Bailiffs of Jersey and Guernsey: *'The*

[46] 10 March 1942 Hedwig Bercu from New Street to Cannon Tower, St Helier; 9 Oct. 1942 Margarete and Hans Hurban to Aimland, Park Estate, Georgetown, St Clement. Clifford Orange's note stated 'as she was registered as a Jewess it was essential that she should obtain and produce the written consent of the Field Command before the change could be effected'; 10 April 1942 Samuel Selig Simon from James Street, St Helier to Battersea, Grand Vaux, St Helier (JAS GEN/3/1940); Also on 4 Nov. 1942 Edmund and Marianne Blampied form Baymont, St Aubin to Keehong, Route Orange, St Brelade (JAS GEN/1/1941).

Property of Jews ... I request that you give directions to the competent department that the compulsory auction sales of furniture or effects belonging to Jews are not to be carried out until further notice'.[47]

On 14 May 1942 an Oberleutnant on behalf of the Standort-Kommandantur in Guernsey requested precise details on the number of registered Jews and Jewish Undertakings in Guernsey. The Nebenstelle replied on 26 May, declaring that only two Jews were resident and confirmed that no Jewish businesses were operating in the island. They noted however that Henry Edward Duquemin, the husband of Elisabet Duquemin a registered Jew, was running a shop. No mention was made of Therese Steiner and Auguste Spitz, who together with Marianne Grunfeld, who had been uncovered had been deported in the previous month. Significantly this is the only surviving correspondence indicating the direct involvement of the military command arm of the German occupying forces in the implementation of measures against the islands Jews.[48]

The Seventh Order

'The Seventh Order relating to measures against Jews' was registered in Guernsey on 16 May 1942 and Jersey on 9 May 1942 as Regulation and Order No 573. This Order redefined the definition of a Jew as contained in the first paragraph of the Third Order. *'Any person having at least three grandparents of pure Jewish blood shall be deemed to be a Jew. A grandparent having been a member of the Jewish religious community shall ipso jure be deemed to be of pure Jewish blood'*. The order also made reference to *'the Order of 13 August 1941 concerning the confiscation of wireless sets belonging to Jews'* stating that this order should also apply to any Jews declaring themselves under the revised definition of the Seventh Order.

The Feldkommandant wrote to the Bailiff requiring this order to be registered in the Royal Court but not published in the 'Jersey Evening Post'. The Attorney-General instructed Clifford Orange to *'take such action as the attached Seventh Order concerning measures against the Jews ....may necessitate'*. Orange immediately published the Order in the 'Jersey Evening Post'. However on 16 May the Feldkommandant wrote to the Bailiff to protest that the Order had been published contrary to his instructions: *'I did not require the ... Orders to be published in the*

[47] Greffier of Guernsey, Orders of German Command 1940-1945. A slightly different translation is in the file, Island of Jersey, AO, Orders relating to measures against Jews, GEN/3/1940.

[48] YV, Guernsey papers, Series 0.9

press as you arranged. The few persons concerned were to have been notified with regard to the Order personally.... I request that in future you will see that only those Orders from the Official Journal are published if I order the publication "in German and English"'[49]

The Eighth Order

'The Eighth Order relating to measures against Jews' was registered in the Royal Court of Guernsey on 30 June 1942. It required that Jews over six years of age must at all times in public wear a six-pointed yellow star inscribed with the word '*Jew*' in black characters. The star was to be sewn in a visible place on the left side of the coat.[50] However the Order was not registered in Jersey seemingly as a result of the intervention of the Bailiff, and Attorney-General. A note in the Bailiff's hand, dated 15 June 1942, pinned to a copy of the proposed Eighth Order has survived in the Bailiff's wartime files. This small note reads '*visited Dr Casper with the Attorney-General – We advised that this order should not be registered or put into execution. Dr Casper agreed I should take no further action at present*'. There are no references to this Order in Clifford Orange's Aliens Office file.[51]

On 15 June in reference to the Eighth Order, Dr Casper wrote to the Nebenstelle in Guernsey requiring confirmation of the numbers of Jews were in the island and details of how many Jewish stars were needed. The matter was one of urgency and Dr Casper required a reply within five days.[52] The Nebenstelle asked the Guernsey Inspector of Police for a list of registered Jews. The Acting Inspector of Police provided the required list, noting Elisabet Duquemin, Elda Brouard and Annie Wranowsky.[53] A hand written draft of a communication between the Nebenstelle and the Feldkommandantur in Jersey dated 17 June also records the names of the known Jews. However this notes indicates that

[49] JAS File B/A/W30/98

[50] Marking Jews with a star had been first muted in 1938: see Raul Hilberg, Perpetrators Victims Bystanders. The Jewish Catastrophe 1933-1945 (London, 1993), p.15.

[51] Bailiff of Jersey, files BA/W30/96; Deputy Edward le Quesne who does not note the Bailiff's intervention in relation to the Eighth Order on 15 June, records in his dairy entry of the same date 'The Bailiff was very upset today by reason of the anonymous letters he has received. The letters principally criticise the attitude the [Superior] Council has adopted in regard to the German order compelling the handing in of all wireless sets. The criticism is not only foolish but also grossly unfair. The Bailiff has humbled himself to a greater extent than many of us would have wished in an attempt to get the order withdrawn.'

[52] YV, Papers on Guernsey, Series 0.9.

[53] Therese Steiner, Auguste Spitz and Marianne Grunfeld (who had not registered but had been uncovered as a Jew) had been deported from Guernsey on 21 April 1942 to their eventual deaths at Auschwitz-Birkenau.

Annie Wranowsky of Sark had been given time to prove that she was not a Jew as the note *records 'is not a Jew ?'.*[54]

On 17 June, despite the intervention of Coutanche with regard to the registration of the Order in Jersey, Dr Casper wrote to the Higher SS and Police Leader's at their headquarters in Paris noting, *'I have asked the States of Jersey and Guernsey to register the Eighth Order ... to make this the law of the islands'.* Dr Casper listed the number of Jews in both islands by nationality, omitting Annie Wranowsky and asked for confirmation of whether British registered Jews should wear a yellow star in addition to the Jews of other nationalities. He concluded by requesting that the required number of yellow six pointed stars emblazoned with the word *'Jew'* in English should be sent from France.[55]

On 19 June the Nebenstelle telexed Jersey ordering six Jewish stars for the two remaining registered British Jews.

On 30 June the Bailiff of Guernsey instructed the Greffier to register the Eighth Order in the Royal Court. The Order was translated into English and the Greffier noted in his file that copies had been sent to Duquemin and Brouard.[56]

On 23 August Dr Casper advised that the stars had not yet arrived. A hand written copy of a message from the Nebenstelle to the Feldkommandantur in Jersey dated 28 December again noted that the stars have not arrived and asked if any decision had been made on whether or not British Jews should be required to wear them. A further letter from Dr Casper to the Nebenstelle dated 5 January 1943 once again noted that the stars had not arrived but continued ominously that this matter was no longer of significance *'as the deportation of the Jews is in sight'.*

The Ninth Order

'The Ninth Order', registered in Guernsey on 21 August 1942 and Jersey on 15 August 1942 as Regulation and Order No 678 banned Jews from places of public entertainment, restricted their shopping hours to

[54] YV, Papers on Guernsey, Series 0.9.

[55] Raul Hilberg, Destruction of the European Jews (New York, 1985), p.634 in relation to the Jewish star order in France stated 'After consultation with the Foreign Office, the following nationalities were determined as safe targets for the measure: Reich, Polish, Dutch, Belgium, French, Croat, Slovakian and Romanian.' These would have been the only Jewish stars in occupied Europe with the word 'Jew' printed in English.

[56] Greffier of the States of Guernsey, File Orders of German Command 1940-1945; A hand written note of the Nebenstelle dated 28 July 1942 states that RVI Zachau was informed that the stars had been ordered: YV, Papers on Guernsey, Series 0.9.

between 3.00pm and 4.00pm and again, in addition to imprisonment and a fine, listed internment in a camp for Jews as a penalty for infraction.

The Bailiff of Jersey received orders from Dr Casper to notify all Jews of the contents of the Ninth Order in writing. The Attorney-General delegated the matter to Clifford Orange providing him with 12 copies of the Order. Orange noted *'A copy was duly handed to each person affected as directed'.*

The Feldkommandantur in Guernsey also required the civilian authorities in Guernsey to confirm that they had notified the two remaining registered Jews of the terms of the order. A further confirmation was required by Dr Casper who wrote to the Bailiff of Guernsey on 3 September asking for details of which Jews had been notified of the restrictions on entering restaurants and places of entertainment included in the Order.[57]

Registration of the Orders in Sark

The first nine Orders were registered by the Seneschal of Sark. On receipt of the Orders from the German authorities the Bailiff of Guernsey instructed his Greffier to send copies to William Carre, Seneschal of Sark. For example, on 21 August the Bailiff instructed the Greffier in respect of the Ninth Order:

> *'I enclose for registration in the Records and transmission to the Seneschal of Sark, copies of Vobif no. 69, containing the Ninth Order regarding measures against the Jews, dated 8.7.1942. Kindly communicate in writing to the Jews concerned a copy of the Order for their information and guidance.'*

The Final Orders

The 'Ordonnance du 2 December 1942' was registered in the Royal Courts of Guernsey on 27 January 1943 and of Jersey on 9 January 1943 as Regulation and Order 787. This Order related to the forfeiture of German nationality of German Jews living abroad and the seizure of their assets. The order would only strictly have applied to Margarete Hurban but it is possible that Hedwig Bercu was re-categorised as a German as most of the references to her after she went into hiding in 1943 (see below) refer to her as a stateless person.

[57] JAS, file, Aliens Office, Island of Jersey - Orders relating to measures against Jews, GEN/3/1940; YV, Guernsey papers, Series 0.9.

The 'Ordonnance du 15 September 1943 (Polonais)' was registered in the Royal Courts of Guernsey on 26 October 1943 and of Jersey on 23 October 1943 as Regulation and Order 941. This Order related to matters concerning Polish Jews.

'The Ordonnance du 15 September 1943 (Boheme et Moravie)' was also registered in the Royal Courts of Guernsey on 26 October 1943 and of Jersey on 23 October 1943 as Regulation and Order 942. This Order related to matters concerning Bohemian and Moravian Jews.

The marking of the Registration cards of registered Jews

The Orders against the Jews were supplemented by other antisemitic measures. On 12 March 1941, after receiving instructions from his superiors in St Germain, the Feldkommandant instructed the Bailiff of Jersey to include the registration cards of Jews with the Registration files for Aliens:

> *'The filing cards of all Jewish persons are to be specially marked and this marking is to consist of a large red J in a conspicuous position and the cards are also to have a red cross strip ... At the same time I would like you to inform me as to the nationality of all Jewish persons'.*

The Bailiff passed the instruction to Clifford Orange who on 17 March confirmed that the cards had been marked and provided a list detailing the nationalities of the 11 registered Jews.

The Bailiff of Guernsey received similar instructions from the German authorities on 17 March.[58] The Bailiff instructed Inspector Sculpher to implement the Order who confirmed on 21 March that the registration cards of Therese Steiner and Auguste Spitz had been marked as required and pointing out that there were two other Jews who were British nationals by marriage.[59]

The confiscation of wireless sets from registered Jews

Although wireless sets were confiscated from the general population in 1942, those belonging to registered Jews were confiscated in the previous year under the 'Order concerning the withdrawal of wireless sets of Jews' of 13 August 1941. On 2 September, the Feldkommandant notified the Bailiff that the Order, *'must either be registered and published in German and English or all Jews must be notified individually'*. The

[58] Therese Marks had died on 10 Dec. 1940.

[59] YV, Guernsey papers. Series 0.9.

Bailiff annotated the Feldkommandant's letter: *'Mr Orange has been asked to deal with each Jew individually'.*[60] Accordingly Clifford Orange instructed each registered Jew to account to him personally in relation to compliance with this Order. On 11 September Clifford Orange reported to the Bailiff that Nathan Davidson, John Jacobs and Hyam Goldman had handed in their radio sets and confirmed all other registered Jews had declared that they did not own radio sets. Orange noted, *'A record of their statements has been kept in my file'.*[61] The radios were to be kept 'in proper trusteeship' by Orange. However Orange on 14 March 1942 noted, *'German soldiers came to fetch the Wireless sets which belong to Jews and had been deposited with me. A written order to take away the sets, addressed to the Bailiff, was produced and receipted by the soldier in charge'.*

Anti-Semitic propaganda

As another line of attack designed to stimulate antisemitism, the German authorities ordered the local newspapers to publish antisemitic articles. As one example the 'Jersey Evening Post' printed an article entitled *'Jewish-Bolshevist Danger'* on 27 April 1942.[62] Another in November 1943 entitled *'Jewry in the U.S.A.'* expounded Nazi ideology claiming that Jewish organisations in the U.S., *'doubtless exert the greatest influence on the [US] Government'* and *'dominate the [American] public by their influence of the film, theatre and press'.*

The German authorities also ordered local cinemas to screen antisemitic films, such as *Jew Suss* which was shown with English subtitles at Wests Cinema in Jersey and the Regal Cinema in Guernsey in October 1941. Peter Hassall, later deported from Jersey under the German *Night and Fog* decree, after having failed in an attempt to escape from the island, remembered watching *Jew Suss* at Wests cinema. His unpublished moving account of his suffering at the hands of the Nazis in occupied Europe and the tragic deaths of his co-escapees also includes his recollection of the screening of *Jew Suss*:

> *'The final scene in Jew Suss depicted the German damsel struggling to protect her virtue, while the Aryan prototype ran up dozens of castle steps. This part of the film elicited cries of admiration from the German audience and their local female*

---

[60] JAS File B/A/W30

[61] Radio sets were confiscated from the general Island population under orders received from Paris in June 1942, Casper: Remembrances.

[62] Jersey Evening Post, 7 Oct. 1941; Articles on 'Jewish Bolshevism' were common throughout Germany and occupied Europe as part of the general program to stimulate antisemitism.

> *companions. The film ended in thunderous applause, when the Jew met his end. It was a gourmet feast for anti-Semitic's minds, and there had to have been a few of them in the audience, given the thunderous applause at the film's conclusion, as well as their remarks on the way out. I hate to admit that I came away from the hateful film somewhat influenced by it, however, the Germans' conduct against the handful of Jews remaining on the island, quickly washed away any anti-Jewish sentiments I may have unconsciously harboured through the vile film. Dennis [Audrain] had accompanied me to the film, and on the way out of the cinema he remarked, 'It's no wonder that the Germans hate Jews when they are fed a steady diet of that stuff'*[63]

Effects of the Orders on the registered Jews

The implementation of the anti-Semitic Orders in the islands had a substantial effect on the lives of the registered Jews as each measure cumulatively placed further restrictions of their freedom, singling them out from the rest of the community. For example, Samuel and Beatrice Simon's great-granddaughter remembered that they lived in a '*terrible state of fear*', especially after they had received a deportation notice. Their actual deportation having been delayed due to Samuel's poor state of health.[64] They were traumatised by the special curfew imposed upon Jews, and indeed such was their state of fear that they kept their curtains closed all day. Shortly before Samuel's death the Simons moved to their daughter Ella's home at Langley Park, St Helier. Samuel died on 7 November 1943, his cause of death is recorded in the St Saviour's Parish register as '*senile myocarditis, cardiac failure*'. He was is buried, not in either of the Jewish graveyards but at St Saviours parish churchyard.

Elisabet Duquemin of Guernsey remembers, *'Every day, for a year and a half until I was deported to a German concentration camp, I lived in fear and terror. I was in trauma all the time. Every day I was frightened,*

---

[63] The 'Night and Fog' (Nacht und Nebel) decree had been promulgated in Dec., 1941; Peter Hassall, Dennis Audrain and Maurice Gould attempted to escape from Jersey in a small boat in May 1942. Audrain drowned in the attempt. Hassall and Gould were deported to German occupied Europe. Gould died through ill-treatment in Oct. 1943 in Wittlich, Germany; his remains were returned to Jersey in 1997. Peter Hassall lives today in Canada; his memoirs are to be published.

[64] Statement to author March 1997; Simon's great-granddaughter visited their house at Grand Vaux, St Helier every Saturday to deliver firewood. Samuel Simon was only given consent to move to this address by Dr Casper on 10 April 1942: see Island of Jersey, AO, Orders relating to measures against Jews, GEN/3/1940.

and did not know if they would take me away, or my baby daughter, or my husband'.[65]

Many of the registered Jews were under constant financial strain as they were unable to earn a living and provide for their families. Gradually, as their circumstances deteriorated, some were forced to move home and to sell their few remaining possessions. Nathan Davidson, his grocery business having been forcibly closed and been forced to move home was left with no means maintaining his family. On 18 January 1943 he pathetically notified Clifford Orange that he had sold his confiscated wireless set and asked Orange to hand it over to the purchaser, a German officer.[66]

Mr and Mrs Nathan Davidson had already been notified of their imminent deportation but the strain was clearly too much and Nathan Davidson was admitted to St Saviour's Mental Institution on 25 February 1943. He died there on 29 February 1944, the St Saviour's Parish register listing his cause of death as '*maniacal exhaustion, insanity*'.[67]

Victor Emanuel committed suicide by hanging at his home on 9 April 1944 and is also buried at St Saviour's cemetery. The coroner recorded a verdict of '*suicide whilst of unsound mind*'.[68]

Those who registered as Jews in 1940 simply did not foresee the dreadful consequences of their declarations. Esther Pauline Lloyd, separated from her husband and children having been deported alone solely because she was a registered Jew, wrote in her diary from Compiegne, a transit and internment camp near Paris: '*6 May 1943 - never shall I be honest again if I had not declared myself this wouldn't have happened - its dreadful*'.[69]

Measures leading to Deportation

In mainland Europe the Final Solution had begun in earnest and massive numbers of Jews had already been murdered in the eastern zones of Occupied Europe.[70] On 20 January 1942 Reinhard Heydrich, the chief of

---

[65] Solomon Steckoll, The Alderney Death Camp (London. 1982); The Duquemin family were deported to internment camps not concentration camps on 13 Feb. 1943.

[66] Island of Jersey, AO, Orders relating to measures against Jews, GEN/3/1940.

[67] JAS, Law Officers Files DZ; St Saviour's Mental Institution records.

[68] Jersey Evening Post, 12 April 1944

[69] Esther Pauline Lloyd Internment camp diaries, copies in possession of author; The first Jews (mainly non-French nationals) to be deported from France had been held at Compiegne in the months leading up to their transportation to Auschwitz-Birkenau on 27 March 1942.

[70] The Einsatzgruppen had already murdered large numbers of Jews in Lithuania and Russia, Einsatzgruppen unit A alone having been responsible for the deaths of over 200,000 Jews in Lithuania between July and November 1941. Mobile gassing vans had been brought into use in

the Reich Security Main Office (Reichssicherheitshauptamt) headed the list of Nazi officials involved in the Final Solution who attended the Wannsee Conference held near Berlin aimed at formalising the extermination of European and Soviet Jewry. The minutes of this conference listed the Jews of Europe country by country; the eleven million noted included the 330,000 Jews in Britain as part of the planned program of extermination.[71]

Returning to the arena of the Channel Islands, the Germans began to tighten measures against the Jews in the islands at the beginning of 1942. Numerous lists were ordered to be complied listing both registered Jews resident in the islands and those who had evacuated. Enquiries were instigated into suspected Jews and in April 1942 the first deportations of resident Jews took place, followed in February 1943 with the deportation of many of the British Jews.

The Higher SS and Police Leaders in Paris ordered Dr Casper to report the number of Jews resident in the islands. In his report dated 17 June 1942 Dr. Casper listed the registered Jews remaining in the islands subsequent to the deportation of Therese Steiner, Auguste Spitz and Marianne Grunfeld who had been uncovered as a Jew:

In Jersey:
7 British nationals
1 Egyptian national
1 German national (this is a hand-written correction)
2 Romanian nationals (also a hand-written correction)
In Guernsey:
2 British nationals (again a hand-written correction).

The list does not include Annie Wranowsky of Sark who was seemingly attempting to prove that she was not a Jew.

The final lists of Jews provided to the Germans

In September 1942 Hitler ordered the mass deportation of non-island born British subjects from the Channel Islands. Oaths sworn after the war by Alexander Coutanche and Clifford Orange (referred to below)

Poland in October 1941. Mass gassings begun in December 1941 at Chelmno death camp resulted in the deaths of 40,000 Jews and Gypsies in just 44 days.

[71] YV, Papers of Guernsey, Series 0.9; Göring authorised Reinhard Heydrich chief of the Reich Security Main Office to prepare a plan for the Final Solution on 31 July 1941, Nuremberg Trials Doc. PS-710 cited in Hilberg, Perpetrators, Victims Bystanders, p.18; Proposals for deportation of Jews from France were first muted in autumn 1941 and authorised by Hitler in Nov. 1941. Mass deportation began in March and July 1942.

state that after this date the civilian authorities in Jersey refused to supply further lists of the resident population to the Feldkommandantur.

On 17 October 1942 Dr Casper wrote to the Controlling Committee in Guernsey and the Bailiff of Jersey requesting a list of those Jews who had left the islands before the Occupation. On 20 October Jersey's Attorney-General instructed Clifford Orange to compile the list but his instruction carried a caveat: *'a full return is impossible, as no information exists upon which to base it. But since the Occupation, declarations have, I believe, been made to you by legal representatives of absentee Jews (or persons believed to be Jews) regarding the property of those persons'.*[72]

On 22 October 1942 John Leale, President of the Guernsey Controlling Committee informed the Nebenstelle stating that the Inspector of Police could not supply a list: *'I beg to inform you that prior to the Occupation Police have no record of Jews resident in Guernsey'*. A footnote added *'Apart from the Police no other States Department has any information concerning Jews'*.

Whilst there are occasional references, particularly with regard to the search for undeclared Jews or those in hiding, the primary source files and diaries of the civilian authorities in Jersey and Guernsey contain little information relating to the islands' Jews after October 1942. The Jersey Law Officers file 'Jewish Undertakings etc' concludes on 21 October 1942. The Jersey Aliens Office file 'Orders relating to Measures against Jews', with the exception of a complaint from Esther Lloyd dated 17 September 1944, concludes on 20 October 1942 and the Jersey Aliens Office Registration and Identification of Persons diary closes on 10 October 1942. The correspondence involving the civilian authorities in Guernsey contained in the file at Yad Vashem ends on 22 October 1942. Similarly the Controlling Committee files provide few further references.[73] The further anti-Jewish orders were registered in the islands Royal courts but after October 1942 the Feldkommandantur appears to have dealt with matters concerning Jews more directly rather than through the civilian authorities.

The deportation of 21 April 1942

The deportation of Therese Steiner, Auguste Spitz and Marianne Grunfeld from Guernsey on 21 April 1942 constituted one of the first

[72] YV, Papers of Guernsey Series 0.9. and Island of Jersey, AO, Orders relating to measures against Jews, GEN/3/1940.
[73] GAS File CC 3-20.

deportations of Jews from Western Europe leading ultimately to Auschwitz-Birkenau.

Marianne Grunfeld was born in Katowice, Poland in 1912. She came to England in 1937 to study horticulture at Reading University. In 1939, on completion of her studies, after responding to an advertisement in an agricultural journal, Grunfeld obtained employment at Duvaux Farm in Guernsey , the home of Edward Ogier, a former member of the States of Guernsey.[74] The Ogier family and Marianne Grunfeld clearly became close and her name appears on a number of occasions in the Duvaux Farm visitors book. The final tragic reference of Christmas Day 1942 notes '*Toasted our dear Marianne Grunfeld, ... and all other evacuees*'. The Ogiers were unaware that Marianne Grunfeld together with her co-deportees Therese Steiner and Auguste Spitz had probably already been murdered at Auschwitz-Birkenau.

Before the Occupation Marianne Grunfeld registered as an alien with the Guernsey Police. In August 1940, after the islands fell under Occupation, she was included as one of over 400 aliens in a list provided to the Germans by the Controlling Committee. She registered in October 1940 under the German imposed legislation requiring all islanders to apply for an identity card, but did not register as a Jew under the first anti-Jewish Order of that month.[75]

On 17 April 1942 Marianne Grunfeld was interrogated at the Nebenstelle for the second time in 12 months. She was warned for deportation on 20 April but this was delayed for one day due to air raids on the French ports.[76] Edward Ogier, her employer, tried unsuccessfully to appeal obtaining a letter of introduction to the Feldkommandantur from John Leale, the President of the Controlling Committee.[77] Reverend Douglas Ord, a Guernsey Methodist minister, noted in his diary on 18 April, *'a friend [presumably Ogier] stopped me outside Grand Lodge, the Civilkommandantur [sic] to vent his rage and sorrow. He had gone to appeal for a girl employee who is only just within the forbidden degrees of Jewish birth and is to be carried off. The officials listened to*

[74] Special exception to the general immigration rules was granted to allow Grunfeld to travel to Guernsey: author's telephone conversation with William Bell, Sept. 1997 (author of I Beg to Report).

[75] The visitors book remains at Duvaux Farm; YV, Papers of Guernsey series 0.9; Guernsey Museum Archive, Registration files for population of Guernsey; The list of over 400 aliens in Guernsey as at 1 June 1940 was supplied to the Nebenstelle on 27 August 1940

[76] Anthony M. Arrol, The Best of It (Williams and Wardley, Guernsey, 1956), p.36.

[77] Ogier's letter of introduction is dated 18 April 1942

the arguments he put but were powerless to resist the inhuman decree of the Nazi Frankenstein'.[78]

It has been suggested that a fellow female worker who was also resident at Duvaux Farm may have denounced Marianne Grunfeld, but there is no evidence to support this hypothesis. Marianne may have been identified from the August 1940 list of aliens, however she was most likely identified from a list of '*key aliens*' supplied to the Feldkommandantur by Guernsey's Controlling Committee on 30 October 1941. 'Grunfeld' would have easily been identified by the Feldkommandantur as a Jewish surname. Furthermore the list of 'key aliens' also names Therese Steiner and Millicent McGahy who were also both deported from Guernsey on 21 April 1942 . Millicent McGahy was a Guernsey born non-Jew who had acquired American nationality through marriage.[79]

Auguste Spitz, born in Austria on 29 August 1901, had arrived in Guernsey in 1937. On 4 June 1940, prior to the Occupation, she was interned as an enemy alien. After release Spitz was employed as a domestic at the Castel Hospital. She registered as a Jew under the First Order of 23 October 1940 and registered in the following week under the all island identity card legislation.[80]

Therese Steiner was born in Austria on 24 February 1916. She qualified as a dental nurse in Vienna and in an effort to escape rising anti-Semitism in Austria went to England to take up a nursing position with Edgar Potts a dentist in Kent. However as war broke out in 1939 the Potts family moved to Sark and Therese Steiner became nanny to the Potts' children. In the following year Edgar Potts returned to his dental practice in England leaving his wife in Sark. Subsequently Marjorie Potts, and her two children accompanied by Therese Steiner moved to Guernsey. As the Occupation loomed, Mrs Potts and her children returned to England but Therese as an Austrian 'enemy alien' was unable to travel. [81] On 4 June 1940 she was interned under the Home

[78] GAS, Files of Controlling Committee (CC), CC 3-20; Priaulx Library, Guernsey, Rev. Douglas Ord Occupation Diary.

[79] GAS, File CC 3-20 letter from Leale to Feldkommandantur, 30 Oct. 1941; A list of all aliens resident in Guernsey had been submitted by the Bailiff to the Feldkommandantur on 29 Sept. 1941. The subsequent list of 30 Oct. 1941 was in response to the Feldkommandantur's request to be notified of the 'Key Persons' contained within the list of 29 Sept. It is possible that this request from the Feldkommandantur may have been precipitated by another letter dated 7 Oct. 1941 from the Controlling Committee to the Feldkommandantur seeking guidance on how to register newly arrived aliens; Millicent McGahy (nee Anderson) was born in Guernsey but had gained American nationality through marriage to Arthur William McGahy; they were not Jewish.

[80] GAS, Registration files.

[81] Prof. Karl Steiner interview with author June 1998

Office 'enemy alien' regulations. On 25 June Therese Steiner and other internees were released and she took up employment as a nurse at Castel Hospital. She registered as a Jew and completed a general identity card registration form on 30 October 1940.[82]

Ernest Plevin, a Police Clerk Sergeant in Guernsey during the Occupation, remembers:

> '... *Guernsey Police were ordered to advise specified Jews to report to Police Headquarters. I was to instruct them to pack their bags and report to the designated German authority.*
>
> *I DO [sic] remember - well - Therese coming into the office, where I conveyed to her the instructions given to the Guernsey Police by the German Military Authorities.*
>
> *Therese became extremely distressed, bursting into tears, and exclaiming that I would never see her again.*'[83]

In a subsequent letter Plevin added: '*The relationship between deportees and Guernsey Police, was always, to my knowledge, good. Police involvement in deportations was rarely more than carrying out orders given by the occupying forces – such as conveying a message to the deportee. At no time were the Guernsey Police permitted to enter the White Rock area*'.[84]

The night before their deportation Therese Steiner and Auguste Spitz visited their friend Elisabet Duquemin, a fellow registered Jewish refugee from Vienna. Elisabet Duquemin remembered: '*They had a paper with them from the Germans that they had to report the next morning to be taken away to France and were in a terrible state of anxiety. They borrowed a suitcase from me and I never saw the poor girls again*'.[85] Reverend Douglas Ord confirmed their state of anxiety: '*When I last spoke with her [Therese Steiner] she had Orders to go to France. She was in great distress and seemed to feel that her feet were now set upon her Via Dolorosa. I did what I could to comfort her but what can you say or do?*'[86]

---

[82] GAS, Registration files; A diary entry for 25 April 1941 in the Jersey AO general diary notes that a 'Miss Steiner, Miss Traumer and Mr and Mrs Schultz reported returning to Guernsey - certificates issued'. It is probable that this was Therese Steiner.

[83] Guernsey Evening Press, Maj E. Parks file on Jews during the Occupation, letter from Plevin, 27 Jan. 1991.

[84] Ibid., letter from Plevin, 21 Feb. 1991; White Rock was a restricted German controlled zone at the harbour.

[85] Statement of Elisabet Duquemin to Steckoll and cited in The Alderney Death Camp, p.126.

[86] Priaulx Library, Guernsey, Rev. Douglas Ord, Occupation diary, entry 4 March 1943.

Steiner, Spitz and Grunfeld were deported on 21 April 1942 together with Millicent McGahy. Barbara Newman, a fellow nurse at Castel Hospital, accompanied Therese Steiner to the Weighbridge, St Peter Port on the day of her deportation. There they met Auguste Spitz and Marianne Grunfeld. The four women were together for approximately 30 minutes before Steiner, Spitz and Grunfeld entered the departure area to board the boat for France. This area was guarded by Germans and Barbara Newman was not allowed to accompany the deportees to the quay.[87]

The Ogier family were visited after the war by Arthur and Millicent McGahy. The couple stated that they had been deported from Guernsey with Marianne Grunfeld. When in France they had all been required to find their own accommodation. Grunfeld had been ordered to wear a Jewish star at all times which she used to hide under her lapel when going out or looking for work. They had been cared for by nuns at one time before Grunfeld was transported by train with other Jews.[88]

By 4 June, archive documents confirm that Steiner, Spitz and Grunfeld were resident in Laval. Spitz and Grunfeld were living at the Hospice Saint-Louis in Laval, a hospice run by the Evron order of nuns. Therese

---

[87] The Registration Forms for Marianne Grunfeld, Therese Steiner, Auguste Spitz and Millicent McGahy are each marked 'To France P.R.177 21 April 1942'. On 22 April 1942 (the day after their deportation) Rittmeister von Oettingen in Guernsey wrote to the Controlling Committee requesting another 'lists of all foreigners within the Bailiwick of Guernsey, according to the latest position'. A list was sent by John Leale on 15 May 1942 but this list does not include Arthur William McGahy, a naturalised American, his Guernsey born wife, Millicent or their son Roy (born 1929). The McGahy's did appear on lists of aliens including Americans that had been supplied to the Feldkommandantur in 1940 and on 29 Sept. 1941. As an American national, Arthur William McGahy was arrested and taken into custody by the German authorities on 2 Jan. 1942 and he may therefore have been deported before 15 May 1942, probably at the same time as his wife Millicent: Barbara Newman, telephone conversation with author, 3 July 1997.

[88] Miss Dennis's statement to the author, April 1997 and Guernsey Evening Press article by Maj E. Parks, 28 May 1991. An analysis of the lists of American nationals identifies the 'couple' as Millicent McGahy and husband Arthur William McGahy: see GAS File CC 3-20.

One detail of this story is however inaccurate as Miss Dennis recounted that the couple had stated their destination as Paris rather than Laval. However as previously stated the Jewish star Order whilst issued on 29 May 1942 did not come into effect until 7 June and Marianne Grunfeld was noted as being already resident in Laval by 4 June. The reference to being cared for by nuns further confirms the location as Laval.

An uncorroborated account (see Guernsey Evening Press archive, Maj. E. Parks file on Jews during the Occupation: Notes on telephone interview with Mrs Mauger, June 1992 and the account of Mrs Whale cited in Bell, I Beg to Report, p.167) claims that after arrival in St Malo, Steiner and Spitz, but not Grunfeld, were held for two to three weeks under guard at a house in Avranches, before being taken away by two SS officers during the night. However, Spitz's French Registration Certificate and Identity Card list her various addresses as, 11 Sept. 1937, Hillside, Castel, Guernsey; 25 June 1938 and 11 Sept. 1940, Manora Albecq, Castel, Guernsey; undated, Castel Hospital, Guernsey. Her only subsequent address is noted as rue Echelle-Marteau and there is no note of any address in Avranches. This must cast considerable doubt on the accuracy of this account.

Steiner, having obtained employment as a nurse had moved to a residential address at rue Echelle-Marteau. Their names appear on two lists of Jews in the Department of Mayenne drawn up as part of the measures to enforce the Yellow Star Order in the region. Austrian/German and Polish Jews were required to wear the Yellow Star.[89]

Reinhard Heydrich chief of the Reich Security Main Office and SS Obersturmbannführer Adolph Eichmann had ordered large deportations of Jews from France to Auschwitz-Birkenau in early March 1942. These were to be organised by SS Hauptsturmführer Theodor Dannecker, Eichmann's representative for Jewish Affairs in Paris with the operational support of the French Police. The first deportations had taken place on 27 March and mass deportations began in mid July.[90]

Therese Steiner and Auguste Spitz were arrested in Laval on 15 July 1942. Marianne Grunfeld was arrested on the following day. The French file records of Steiner and Spitz are both marked '*deported to an unknown destination*'.

The Reverend Douglas Ord noted in his diary '*In hospital today I learned that that bright and universally respected little nurse Steiner had been taken to France for internment. A letter had come from her saying that she and another girl like her were being taken to Poland*'.[91]

After their arrest in Laval on 15-16 July 1942 Steiner, Spitz and Grunfeld were transported to Angers. The transportation from Angers had originally been scheduled for 17 July but a deportation from

[89] The Order requiring that Jews wear a Yellow Star was issued in Paris on 29 May 1942 but did not come into effect in the region of Mayenne until 7 June 1942; A letter of 25 June 1942 from the Prefecture Regionale d'Angers to the Prefet de la Mayenne confirms that Austrian/German and Polish Jews in the department had been ordered to wear Jewish stars; The list established by the Prefecture of Mayenne dated 2 Dec. 1944 records 70 Jews arrested for deportation in the Department including 13 Jews resident in Laval arrested in the round-ups of 15/16 July. The other records and lists held in the Mayenne archive include the lists of Jews in the district dated 4 June 1942 and 9 June 1942 (by nationality), the Identity Card and Certificate of Registration of Auguste Spitz together with the individual files of Steiner, Spitz and Grunfeld: Archives of Conseil General de la Mayenne, Laval, documents 265W59-63; An analysis of the 4/9 June lists of Jews by profession and nationality shows that Spitz and Grunfeld were unemployed; this may explain why Therese Steiner was living at a residential address whereas Grunfeld and Spitz were in the care of the hospice Saint Louis. The Central Laval archives confirmed that the hospice Saint-Louis was run by the Sisters d'Evron, an order established in the seventeenth century dedicated to the care of the deaf and dumb.

[90] Hilberg, Destruction of the European Jews, pp. 633-9 and Serge Klarsfeld, Le Calendrier de la persecution des Juifs de France 1940-1944 (Paris, 1993).

[91] Priaulx Library Guernsey, The diary of Rev. Douglas Ord, entry for 4 March 1943; The suggestion that Jews were being sent to a new 'Jewish State' in Poland was used as a pretext for deportation to Auschwitz-Birkenau by Higher SS and Police Leader Oberg in his negotiations with the Chief of the French Government Pierre Laval: see Hilberg, Destruction of the European Jews, p. 637.

Bordeaux had been delayed because insufficient '*stateless*' Jews had been rounded up.[92] A telex sent by the Jewish department of the Gestapo in Paris stated that Convoy No.8 departed from Angers-St Laud station on 20 July 1942 at 8:35pm under the command of Lt. Oetterer. Therese Steiner, Auguste Spitz and Marianne Grunfeld were amongst the 824 Jews loaded onto the cattle trucks. The train was routed via Drancy, where 28 Jews were unloaded due to complications over establishing their nationality, and arrived at Auschwitz-Birkenau on 23 July.

Dr Andre Lettich also deported on Convoy No.8 with his wife and five year old son remembers:

> *After arriving at Angers, we were deprived of our valuables and personal mementoes and we were herded together in the small rooms of a seminary, twenty five to thirty a room, the doors were locked with keys.*
>
> *The following day we were taken to the courtyard and put in lorries by our guards and taken to the railway station, where we were put in cattle cars, seventy five to eighty per wagon, the windows and doors hermetically sealed.*
>
> *During the journey, crammed one against another, we suffered terribly from thirst, and we were obliged to sacrifice a small corner of the cattle car for calls of nature.*
>
> *On 23 July at about four clock in the afternoon ... the train stopped and we heard violent bangs as the seals of the wagons were removed. Shouting as usual, the SS, make it clear that everyone must disembark from the carriage with their baggage.*
>
> *They ordered us to stand in ranks of five. It was raining. We were up to our knees in mud. The mud and the rain, the rain and the mud ..., they were to become familiar during more than two years in this remote part of Poland, that Polish doctors said was the most unhealthy part of their country, where typhus, typhoid and malaria were endemic diseases.*

The 390 women in the convoy were issued with identification numbers 10177 to 10566. Due to their age Therese Steiner, Auguste Spitz and Marianne Grunfeld may have been amongst those women who survived the initial 'Selektion' at which those regarded as unsuitable for work were immediately sent to the gas chambers. In transportations documented in the same week in July 1942 most of those immediately

[92] Pierre Laval, Chief of the French Government, had negotiated with Higher SS and Police Leader Oberg with the result that the first deportations were predominantly made up of 'stateless' Jews (including their children) not protected by a foreign power.

gassed were the children, the elderly and the sick.[93] Some of the women deported to Auschwitz-Birkenau at this time were subjected to medical experiments.[94]

Therese Steiner, Auguste Spitz and Marianne Grunfeld may have survived the initial selection, however they did not survive the war. Of convoy No.8 only 14 men and not a single woman are known to have survived the horrors of Auschwitz-Birkenau.[95]

The deportation of 'non-indigenous British Channel Islanders' in September 1942

In late 1941 Adolf Hitler ordered the deportation of non-island born British residents of the Channel Islands in retaliation for the internment of Germans living in Iran. Detailed lists of the mainland born subjects resident in the islands were prepared in September and October but the deportation itself did not take place.

The Reverend Douglas Ord in Guernsey, noted in his diary on 24 September 1941

> *A vile rumour has upset the Island. For some time past the Front Page has been working up a 'hate' on account of the forestalling of the Nazi plans for seizing Iran. It is now said that as a reprisal for the seizure of Nazi agents in Iran all non-Guernsey born males will be deported as hostages. The ages mentioned vary between 18 to 45 and even to 60. What there is in this we do not know. But the fact remains that the German Authorities have asked for some detailed reports on all not island-born.*

The Feldkommandantur also prepared lists of Aliens and Jews in the islands at this time. Clifford Orange noted in the Aliens Office '*12:15pm Mr Mollet, Bailiff's Secretary, brought me a request from German Field Command for four copies of list of aliens, including Jews and Stateless,*

---

[93] On 17 July two transportations of Dutch Jews had arrived at Auschwitz-Birkenau, 1,251 men and 300 women were tattooed and sent to barracks, the remaining 449 were gassed. On 21 July 879 men and 121 women arrived at Auschwitz-Birkenau in a transportation originating from Paris, of these 375 were gassed immediately. (see Gilbert, The Holocaust, p. 376)

[94] Medical experiments on women at Auschwitz-Birkenau were sanctioned at a meeting on 7 July 42: see Martin Gilbert, The Holocaust (Fontana, 1987), p.373.

[95] The R.F. SS transport lists of Convoy 8 at the Panstwowe Muzeum Oswiecim lists No 38 Marianne Grunfeld, profession–worker, nationality-Deutsch R., residence–Laval, No 75 Augusta Spitz, profession–unknown, nationality-Oesterreich, residence–Laval, No 76 Therese Steiner, profession–nurse, nationality–Oesterreich, residence–Laval; SS transportation notice dated 17 Aug. 1942 signed by SS Hauptsturmführer Hans-Dietrich Erns at Angers; Report entitled Convoi No. 8 en date du 20 Juillet 1942: All held at CDJ, Paris; Gilbert, The Holocaust, p. 376.

to be made and delivered by 6 pm on Monday 20 October'. Summary lists including *'copies of lists of registered Jews in Jersey'* were submitted by the Aliens Office on 20 October. [96]

However on 23 January 1942 Jersey Feldkommandant Colonel Knackfuss notified 319 Infantry Division on mainland Europe that the removal of the non-indigenous island population was not an appropriate measure. Knackfuss stated that the presence of 8,000 'influential' Channel Islanders, considered important by the British government were providing a shield discouraging the British government from mounting a military operation to retake the islands.[97] Furthermore transferring the non-indigenous population would prevent their being used in retaliation in the event of English or American measures against Germans. Colonel Knackfuss also noted that his views were shared by other German officials.

In this same letter Knackfuss also made reference to the implementation of another genocidal element of Nazi ideology, ominously noting that the removal of the islands mentally inferior to institutions *'for reasons of population policy ... was particularly desirable and already arranged (about 450 persons)'*. This reference however post-dates Hitler's order to partially wind down the euthanasia of the mentally program in mainland Europe and there is no evidence that Knackfuss's policy was implemented.[98]

One year later during negations of a Swiss proposal for the exchange of prisoners of war Hitler discovered that his order to deport the non-indigenous British Channel Islanders had not been carried out. An inconclusive investigation was ordered to determine why the deportation had not been actioned and in early September 1942 Hitler personally issued direct instructions to deport *'British subjects on the Channel Islands who do not belong to the indigenous people'*.[99] On 15 September 1942 Colonel Knackfuss published a notice of the intended deportation

---

[96] Aliens Office Diary 'Registration and Identification of Persons' 16 Oct 1941; JID, Auslanderlisten –. An Aliens Office list survives based on an Aliens office typed list dated 6 Nov. 1940. This is entitled Auslanderlisten and it has been updated and annotated in a German hand including the marking of a 'J' beside the names of Margarete Hurban and Hedwig Bercu

[97] In 1941 Churchill ordered his defence staff to investigate retaking one of the Channel Islands in 'Operation Attaboy'. The plan was shelved on grounds of the 'negligible' strategic value of the Islands, the resources required and the difficulty of holding on to an Island after capture. In 1942 a plan to retake Alderney, 'Operation Blazing' was considered but again this was shelved. Raids were also considered but 'the necessity of leaving ... would be most discouraging to our own people living there ... and possibly [they] would be the victims of reprisals'.

[98] Bundesarchiv – Military Archives RH 26 319/8 - FK 515 to 319 ID - 23 Jan. 1942; In late summer 1941 Hitler ordered the winding down of the euthanasia of the mentally ill program: see Hillberg, The Destruction of the European Jews, p895

[99] JAS, Bailiff of Jersey Files, BA/L33/1; Alexander Coutanche's oath after Liberation.

in the 'Jersey Evening Post'. Approximately 2,000 non-island born British subjects were deported from Jersey, Guernsey and Sark in the following three weeks.

After the war Alexander Coutanche and Clifford Orange were questioned by British Intelligence officers about their provision of lists of British subjects deported in September 1942. Clifford Orange stated in the draft of an oath to be sworn by him and headed: *'In the matter of German War Crimes and in the matter of Clifford Orange'*:

> *At various times ... the German authorities called for lists ... of various categories of persons registered under the legislation referred to above [The Registration and Identification of Persons Jersey Order 1940]. Amongst such lists was one containing particulars of British subjects resident in the Channel Islands who did not belong to the local population, and another containing particulars of British Regular Officers (Retired) registered as residing in Jersey. Both of these were supplied in November 1941.*
>
> *As from September 1942 when it became obvious the purpose to which lists of persons supplied long before were being put, I refused to supply any further lists to the German authori*ties.[100]

On 12 June 1945 Alexander Coutanche swore a similar oath in which he detailed his efforts to object to the preparation of lists of British subjects for deportation. Bailiff Coutanche testified:

> *'[I] asked whether I could do nothing to stop it [deportation], or at least to delay it. Colonel Knackfuss replied that the Order came from the Führer himself, that no one had the power to vary it in the slightest degree, and that it would be carried out to the letter whatever I might say and do.*
>
> *In view of what was proposed I and any other member of the Islands Government who wished to do so would be entitled to resign.... Colonel Knackfuss replied, without conceding my right to withdraw from the Government, that it was clearly in the interest of the people of Jersey that the government should continue in Office...*
>
> *Subsequently the Attorney General and I obtained from the Feldkommandant a promise that the Evacuation Orders would be served by Members of the German Armed Forces – The*

[100] The Sept. 1942 deportees, however, do not appear to have been drawn exclusively from the lists of British subjects supplied to the German Authorities by the Aliens Office in 1941: Ronald Gould and family deported from Jersey, for example, do not appear on the 1941 list.

Constables only being required to supply a "Guide" for finding the addresses'.[101]

Although the names of a small number of individuals who may have come within the German definition of a Jew appear amongst the lists of those deported in September 1942 there is no evidence to suggest that any were deported specifically because they were Jews.[102]

The Deportation of Jews in February 1943

On 3 October 1942 the Allied forces launched a small scale raid on Sark. 'Operation Basalt' comprised 12 officers and men under the command of Major J. Appleyard. Five Germans were captured and bound. They attempted to escape but a German officer and a private were killed and another soldier captured.

On hearing of this raid Hitler ordered the shackling of 1,400 Allied prisoners captured at Dieppe. As another reprisal, Berlin ordered a further deportation of Channel Islanders comprising specific categories of persons.[103]

On 27 December 1942 the German Military Commander of western occupied Europe sent a telex to the High Command of the Wehrmacht. This document, headed 'secret', ordered that the deportees were to be drawn from specific categories of Channel Islanders including, Jews and high ranking Freemasons; former Officers and reserve Officers; persons with previous convictions; communists and politically suspect persons; those who refused to work; young men without useful employment in the Nazi sense; clergy; leading public figures and wealthy people who might exert an anti-German influence and the inhabitants of Sark not engaged in agriculture. Those islanders remaining in Sark were to be moved away from the coast. Significantly, as far as the deportation of the Jews was concerned, the telex stated that where the person to be deported was the head of a family then the whole family were also to be deported. The telex estimated that without counting family members, about 1,000 islanders would fall within these categories. Furthermore the deportation could be arranged in four weeks.[104]

---

[101] Bailiff of Jersey, BA/L33/1 Oath sworn before Major Francis Haddock 12 June 1945.

[102] Sydney Jewell and William Alfred Benjamin are listed as deported to Biberach and Laufen internment camps in Germany. The Jewells were a prominent Jersey Jewish family dating back to the early nineteenth century with connections in Plymouth where Sydney Jewell was born on 2 Oct.1908. It is known that William Benjamin was repatriated after the War.

[103] Chruickshank, The German Occupation of the Channel Islands, p.240-2.

[104] International Military Tribunal, Nuremberg: Document PS 724.

On 5 January 1943 Dr Casper informed the Nebenstelle in Guernsey: *'The Jewish stars ordered from the Higher SS and Police Leader [in Paris] have not yet arrived. The matter in any case is superseded because the deportation of the Jews is in sight.'* The letter is annotated *'Elda Brouard, Elisabet Duquemin and her family are to be deported.'*

On 10 January Colonel Knackfuss notified the Bailiff of Jersey: *'In virtue of the Orders received from superior Authorities a transportation of individual categories of persons will shortly take place. The list of the persons to be transported will be sent to you as soon as the transportation takes place'.*[105]

On 11 January 1943 notices were sent out by special mail to most intended deportees in Jersey.[106] The notices warned that deportees would be, *'informed, either by special notice or by a notice in the Evening Post newspaper, of the exact time and date when you will have to report at the harbour of St Helier for the purposes of evacuation'.* However, unlike the deportation of British subjects in September 1942, no official notices appeared in the island press and the names of those to be deported were not published.

The civilian authorities were however provided with a list of the intended deportees at least one week before the deportation took place. A 'List of Transportees received from Feldkommandant' dated 6 February 1943 survives in the Jersey Law Officer's files. This list is typed in English and was clearly compiled by the civilian authorities from information received from the Feldkommandantur. [107]

The German authorities after further investigation re-estimated that there were approximately 500 persons in the relevant categories in Jersey, Guernsey and Sark. Intended deportees were interviewed at the Feldkommandantur, as a result of which a number were given exemption from deportation, mostly based on medical grounds. The final list of those to be deported did not include persons from all the designated classes.

On 5 February 1943 the German authorities sent out the final deportation notices by mail warning that transportation would take place on Tuesday, 9 February, this date being a hand written correction over the original printed date of 7 February. The notices stated that deportees must assemble at the Forum Cinema at 2.00pm: *'for ... evacuation to*

---

[105] JAS, Bailiff of Jersey Files, BA/W80 submitted to Superior Council on 13 Jan. 1943. The Law Officers 'List of Transportees received from Feldkommandant' included the names of a number of individuals, including some registered Jews, who were not subsequently deported.

[106] Deportation order of John Jacobs dated 11 Jan. 1943 in possession of his daughter-in-law.

[107] JAS, Law Officers files D/Z.

Germany'.[108] However bad weather delayed the transportation and on 12 February a fault with the engine of the transportation ship resulted in a further delay. On 13 February the deportees finally left for St Malo.[109]

In Guernsey the Bailiff sent out the deportation notices by mail on 3 February. The deportees were scheduled for transportation on 9 February but the departure was delayed initially for 24 hours and then for a further two days.[110] They finally departed on 12 February but had to wait on a train in St Malo until the Jersey deportees arrived on the following day.

Adult male deportees under the age of 64 were initially transported to Lager Laufen in southern Germany. The other deportees were sent to the Lager Compiegne near Paris.[111]

The Nebenstelle's own lists detail the Jews included in the deportation and include notes confirming that each were deported specifically because they were Jews. These lists note:

> To Lager Compiegne:
> Elda Brouard (stated reason for deportation 'Jew')
> Elisabet Duquemin (stated reason for deportation 'Jew')
> Janet Duquemin, aged 18 months (deported as child of Elisabet)
> To Lager Laufen:
> Henry Duquemin (stated reason for deportation 'Wife is a Jew')

The Jersey Feldkommandantur lists note:

> To Lager Compiegne:
> Alfred Bertie Still
> Ruby Ellen Still
> Michael Lewis Still
> John Max Finkelstein
> Esther Pauline Lloyd.[112]

---

[108] Harris, Islanders Deported, p.29; GAS, File FK 13-1; Notice of intended deportation dated 5 Feb.1943 sent to Albert Chardine and still in his possession; One of the intended deportees committed suicide.

[109] Harris, Islanders Deported, p.33.

[110] The Rev. Ord diary, Feb. 1943.

[111] GAS, File FK 13-1 and File FK 12/14.

[112] Michael Still and John Finkelstein whilst listed as having been transported to Compiegne were actually transported to Laufen; The most comprehensive lists of those deported from Jersey, Guernsey and Sark on 13 Feb. 1943 are the German authorities lists of deportees in the Feldkommandantur files at the GAS and the Bailiff's files at the JAS. The Guernsey lists state the reason for deportation in the case of each individual deportee. The lists can be summarised as follows: 40 deportees from Jersey to Lager Laufen; 12 deportees from Jersey to Lager Compiègne; 60 deportees from Guernsey to Lager Laufen; 64 deportees from Guernsey to Lager Compiègne; 2 deportees from Sark to Lager Laufen; 24 deportees from Sark to Lager Compiègne. The Jersey Jews and their families are listed sequentially.

On 20 May, the Channel Island deportees at Compiegne were transferred to Lager Biberach in Germany. On 6 August the younger men initially transferred to Laufen were also transported to Biberach. Seven other men who had been sent to Kreuzberg were transferred to Biberach on 1 August.[113]

John Max Finkelstein, as a Romanian Jew, was singled out for special treatment after his arrival at Laufen and was transported to Tittmoning a few miles away. After several months he was transported by train to Weimar and from there to the nearby Buchenwald concentration camp.[114] Nearly two years later, as the Allied forces approached Buchenwald in early April 1945, the Germans transferred some of the prisoners, including Finkelstein, to Theresienstadt. The majority of those transported were in an appalling physical condition, which combined with the poor sanitary and dietary conditions at Theresienstadt rapidly lead to epidemics. When the Soviet forces finally liberated Theresienstadt on 8 May 1945, Finkelstein was amongst the 17,000 survivors. Due to the disease then prevalent in the camp many of the survivors were unable to leave the camp immediately. Finally Finkelstein was released and was issued with a transit identity card in Lyons on 7 September 1945. He returned to Jersey before 4 January 1946 where he remained until his death in 1972.

Henry Duquemin received his family's deportation order on 4 February 1943. On the same day he wrote a letter of appeal to the Nebenstelle, *'I have this day received a notification from the Bailiff of Guernsey to the effect that my wife and I must hold ourselves in readiness to proceed to an Internment Camp in Germany'*.[115] The Nebenstelle annotated his unsuccessful appeal: '*Wife is a Jew*'. Duquemin was initially transported to Laufen before being transferred to Biberach. Elisabet and Janet were initially transported to Compiegne before their transfer to Biberach.

---

[113] Esther Pauline Lloyd Diaries, in the collection of the Institute of Contemporary History and Wiener Library, London; In March 1944 the Channel Islands Refugee's Committee published the International Red Cross list of those transferred from Compiègne to Biberach on 20 May 1943: Elda Brouard - camp number 10022, Elisabet Duquemin 9999, Janet Duquemin 10075, Alfred Bertee Still 9981, Ruby Ellen Still 10051, Esther Pauline Lloyd 10002. Transferred from Laufen to Biberach in 6 August 1943: Henry Duquemin 1061, Michael Lewis Still 1029: Societe Jersiaise, Deportation Box File.

[114] See PRO FO Claims Dept. File 23/M/1964FO; Claims Department correspondence with the International Tracing Service in Arolsen, Germany, 23 Nov. 1964; Sir Ambrose Sherwill in the foreword to Frank Stroobant, One Man's War (Guernsey, 1988), refers to transfers of men from Laufen to Tittmoning; Finkelstein was transferred at a time when there was increasing pressure from Berlin to include Romanian Jews in the Final Solution.

[115] GAS, File FK/13-1. The letter of appeal was unusually marked indicating that it was sent to RVI Zachau.

Michael Still was transported to Laufen and subsequently to Biberach. His parents Alfred and Ruby Still were transported to Compiegne before their transfer to Biberach.

Elda Brouard was transported to Compiegne then Biberach. The Biberach Camp register records that she was then transported together with other single women from Biberach to Liebenau camp on 2 October 1944.[116]

Esther Pauline Lloyd's husband, who was not Jewish, and their two children were listed on the 'List of transportees received from the Feldkommandant' of 6 February 1943. Due to her husband's claimed ill-health only Esther Lloyd was actually deported. Esther Lloyd was initially transported to Compiegne and then to Biberach.

The Esther Pauline Lloyd internment camp diaries

Esther Pauline Lloyd kept a diary during her internment at Compiegne and Biberach; the two surviving diaries cover the period 7 April to 23 November 1943. They contain almost daily entries and provide a unique insight into the life of a British Jewish internee. The dairies confirm that with the exception of Finkelstein (a Romanian) the other Jewish deportees as British nationals were treated largely in the same way as the non-Jewish Channel Island deportees. They were not separated from the non-Jews and were accommodated in the same barracks.[117]

The diaries detail Esther Lloyd's appeal against her deportation soon after her arrival at Compiegne. On 18 April 1943 she wrote, '*Rain, I feel very depressed, longing for home. The girls sent a letter to Commandant - my name is in it, if nothing happens I shall ask to see him.*'[118]

---

[116] The Biberach Camp Register is deposited at the Library of the Societe Jersiaise.

[117] When considering the diaries it must be noted that Esther Lloyd left Biberach before the contingents of Jewish prisoners of varied nationalities arrived at the camp from Bergen-Belsen. The first contingent comprised approximately 150 predominantly Tripolian Jews who were emaciated and lice infested on arrival; a number had died en-route. The second contingent of Jews from Bergen-Belsen arrived at Biberach on 23 January 1945 and comprised a mix of approximately 130 Austrian, Polish, Dutch, Belgium and Hungarian nationals. A detailed account of the arrival and condition of the Jews transferred from Bergen-Belsen is contained in the report compiled after the liberation of Biberach by the camp leader, Garfield Garland. The Biberach Camp register records the details of each prisoner: JAS Bailiff of Jersey Files, report by Garfield Garland.

[118] The Esther Pauline Lloyd diaries were written with little punctuation. To facilitate the readability of the entries punctuation has been added by the author of this paper where necessary.

Esther Lloyd then sent a letter to the Commandant, a draft of which appears at the end of her first diary:

> *'21 April 1943*
>
> *Sir,*
>
> *Is it possible I could have the favour of an interview at your Bureau on urgent personal affairs. There is no privacy at the camp at all and as I speak practically no German it would have to be done through an interpreter.*
>
> *Thanking you'*

On the same day Lloyd wrote: *'Had lovely letter from Billy and the girls rushed in with news we four were going home. I can't believe it, however, I have started packing and my letter is written ready for Commandant. Mrs G has just had news her son is killed'*. The news of her in imminent repatriation was premature and consequently Lloyd experienced periods of depression frustrated by the slowness of her appeal as it was passed between Jersey, Paris and Berlin. The diaries also reveal her increasing despair at being separated from her husband Billy and children, David and Miriam.

On 28 April 1943 Lloyd wrote:

> *'David's Birthday: its a fine day I expect he will enjoy his party [in Jersey]. I feel very sad at the moment have just had breakfast and we are supposed to be definitely moving on this week [to Biberach]. The outlook is fairly hopeless for me so I suppose I must resign myself to a long absence. It's very hard as life is so aimless, no interest in anything. Why should the other 3 who didn't want to go home go, and me, who would give anything am stuck – it's damnable'.*

After her transfer to Biberach, Lloyd's hopes for repatriation were raised again, she wrote: *'26 June - I had an interview with Garland [Garfield Garland, a Guernsey deportee and Head of Camp] and he had news just come in that my case has gone on to the Neutral Powers so it's very hopeful. T.... and D..... had notes to tell them they can't go back to the islands. Feel hopeful, what joy to leave this terrible place of hateful women and spiteful tongues.'*

Her despondency increased. On 5 August after receiving a letter from her husband, Charles 'Billy' Lloyd, she recorded, *'I get so homesick when I read them. It's dreadful to read Dr Casper has only to say yes to get me home'*.

Billy Lloyd visited the Feldkommandantur in Jersey to appeal for his wife's repatriation. On 27 September Esther Lloyd wrote: *'I had a letter [on] Saturday from Billy saying that at last he has permission for me to go home. I just have to wait for the next transport. I am absolutely down, feel my nerves are giving way. It's too frightful for words, a living nightmare to me who is so sensitive. I keep picturing myself at home'.* Two days later she noted: *'I saw Miss Y today and she said Col. Knackfuss would have to inform Berlin first so I shall have to wait. Please God it will be soon - its pure Hell for me mixing up with all these different people'.*

The diaries contain a number of references to Elisabet Duquemin one of the two registered Guernsey Jews. They were billeted together in the same barrack where Elisabet Duquemin had been elected '*Barrack Leader*'. Lloyd was clearly concerned that this might lead to attention being drawn to the Jewish internees. Duquemin, as Barrack Leader, had restricted access to the showers. Lloyd wrote: *'23 April 1943 -Good Friday, what a day, dull, everyone getting on edge. Mrs Duquemin has resigned, letters and showers for kitchen only. [I] am playing patience as I'm fed up. Mrs Duquemin is chief again'.*

'24 April -never slept, terrible night planning when I get home. At breakfast of which I had none, trouble started over Mrs Duquemin: no showers (what a shame and of course Mrs W said to me [there could be] more trouble for Jews having such a woman as head)'.[119]

The diaries provide a unique insight into the life of the internees revealing the conflicts of personality that arose and the arguments that ensued. They detail daily life, how bartering for goods evolved, and describe the entertainment arranged by internees to occupy their time. On 2 July 1943 Lloyd wrote: '*Parcels English again and 40 cigs [sic]. Got a hand knitted pullover by N C's mother for 50 cigs, have undone it to be re-knitted. Got tin of nescafe for 30 cigs [and] had a good day on whole*'.

The diaries also provide detailed accounts of many important aspects of the internment of the Channel Islanders, including a vivid description of the transfer from Compiegne to Biberach on 20-21 May 1943 and details of thc transfer of the men from Kreuzberg and Laufen in August 1943. Having been taken by train from Compiegne to Paris, Lloyd wrote: *'21 May 1943 - arrived at Strasbourg about 5am and we are here till 2.0. Have just had a bit of food and coffee and have gone in a wooden compartment to sleep ... we saw a lot of French men going away yesterday as prisoners and their wives crying on the platform, all the*

[119] Mrs Elda Brouard, the other registered Jew from Guernsey, has written her name and barrack number in the back of Lloyd's first diary 'Mrs E Brouard 10022 – Z1/122 Compiègne Olse, France'.

soldiers want the war to end ... Started off 2.45 3pm just past Rhine, crossed over bridge, Kehl canal just seen ... Pass through Karlsuhr [sic] ... stopped at Stuttgart, huge station, very busy ... all the soldiers very kind ... arrived Biberach 10.30.'

The diaries reveal that Esther Lloyd became interested in reverting to Judaism. These entries would have posed a considerable risk to her, had they been discovered by the Germans.

> *'29 September - I have completely finished with the Christian religion, the children must leave Sunday school at end of the Xmas Hols [sic]. My wish is that David will grow up with the real Faith, the religion that does help. I wish I had been brought up properly to know everything about [it] and had learnt Hebrew when I had the chance. Well time will tell. I feel very bitter now towards humanity and as for the majority of women they want drowning.'*

Remarkably, Lloyd's appeal was successful and she was repatriated to Jersey on 25 April 1944. [120] After her repatriation and significantly whilst the island was still under German occupation, Esther Lloyd made a complaint to the Bailiff . This complaint is examined in the conclusions section of this paper.

Registered Jews who were not deported

A number of Jews and their dependant family members were ordered for deportation on 13 February 1943 but not subsequently deported. Nathan Davidson, Romanian by birth but a naturalised Egyptian subject, and his non-Jewish wife were on the 'List of intended transportees received from the Feldkommandant' dated 6 February . However, as stated above, he was admitted to St Saviour's Mental Institution in February 1943 where he died a year later.[121]

Although not listed in the list of intended deportees dated 6 February John Jacobs, his non-Jewish wife and children received a notice of their intended deportation on 11 January 1943. John Jacobs was suffering from tuberculosis and was consequently certified as unfit to travel. Initially a German doctor and German officer visited the Jacobs home every week to establish his state of health. Jacobs died in jersey in 1944. After his death his family discovered that he had not taken all his

---

[120] Island of Jersey, AO, Orders relating to measures against Jews, GEN/3/1940.
[121] JAS, Law Officers files D/Z.

prescribed medicine; he had seemingly feared that any recovery would have led to his family's deportation.[122]

Samuel Selig Simon is believed to have received a deportation notice but was not deported due to his poor health. He died on 7 November 1943.[123] Again his name is not included in the list of proposed deportees which seemingly does not include the names of those who had been granted early exemptions.

Annie Wranowsky's documented efforts to prove she was not a Jew likely saved her from deportation to Auschwitz with Steiner, Spitz and Grunfeld in 1942. Wranowsky was a friend of the Dame of Sark and in September 1941 John Leale had notified the Nebenstelle that Wranowsky had become teacher of German at the Sark school, noting: *'which Frau Annie Wranowsky has kindly promised to give free of charge'*. By the time of the deportation of April 1942 Wranowsky had clearly prompted a re-examination of her status as a Jew. An annotation on the Sark copy of the Bailiff's order to register the Seventh Order in Sark in May 1942 noted: *'No Jews known to me - AJR'*. The Nebenstelle's correspondence with the Feldkommandantur in Jersey confirms that Wranowsky status remained unresolved in June 1942 at the time of the registration of the Yellow Star order.[124] However in January 1943 Wranowsky's was ordered for deportation but the Feldkommandantur annotated her deportation order *'German nationality, has Jewish passport and is presently trying to prove her Aryan origin'*.[125] In the third week of April 1943 Wranowsky was granted a permit to travel to Guernsey, the purpose of which was stated as *'to prove her Aryan descent and to visit a dentist'*.[126] It would appear Wranowsky's appeal to prove her *Aryan* status was successful.[127] After the war Annie Wranowsky married her employer Ernold Mason, a retired artist and remained in Sark.

---

[122] John Jacobs' deportation order has been presented by his daughter-in-law to the Imperial War Museum Holocaust Exhibition; Author's interview with Georgina Jacobs, John Jacobs' daughter-in-law March 1997.

[123] Statement of great granddaughter to author, March 1997.

[124] YV, papers of Guernsey Series 0.9. Hand written communication between Nebenstelle to Jersey Feldkommandantur 17 June 1942

[125] GAS, deportation orders, File FK13-1.

[126] GAS, File FK 1.11, List of special travel permits issued to civilians from 14-20 April 1943.

[127] It has been suggested that the Dame of Sark intervened over Wranowsky's deportation. There is however no documentary evidence to support this theory. However their friendship is confirmed by a letter sent by the Dame to Mr Pleul in Guernsey dated 6 Oct 1941 requesting help in obtain German books for the lessons being given to 22 Sark children by Wranowsky does however state 'My friend Frau Wranowsky, whom you know is giving the lessons': GAS File FK 16-4

There are a further group of registered Jews in Jersey, who were not deported and for whom we have no confirmation as to whether or not they or their families received deportation notices.

Marianne Blampied was married to Edmund Blampied the prominent Jersey born non-Jewish artist. Dr Casper wrote that Edmund Blampied was, '*an artist I thought very highly of*', and stated that in May 1943 he had recommended that he be appointed by the States of Jersey to paint the landscapes for a new issue of stamps.[128]

Victor Emanuel was born in Germany but held a British passport. As previously stated, he committed suicide on 9 April 1944.

Hyam Goldman, a British national, was according to one uncorroborated account not deported because the German authorities required his skills as a beekeeper on account of the sugar shortage. Goldman never recovered from his experiences during the Occupation and on 10 October 1950 he was found dead in a water tank at his home.[129] The verdict of the inquest was that having been depressed for some time he had committed suicide by drowning in a water tank, holding his body down with weights. He is buried at the Westmount Jewish Cemetery.

Hedwig Bercu was born in Austria but classified in Dr Casper's letter of 17 June 1942 in his hand-written correction as Romanian. The original uncorrected type script appears to have classified Bercu as German. She had arrived in Jersey on 15 November 1938 with a British visa issued in the same month in the name of Hedwig Bercu-Goldenberg and a foreigner's passport issued in Vienna in September 1938 in the name of Hedwig Bercu. She was also in possession of a Registration card issued in Vienna in May 1937 in the name of Hedwig Goldenberg, this recorded that she was a Romanian national. When she arrived in Jersey before the war her immigration formalities were dealt with by the Immigration Officer, Clifford Orange.[130]

In October 1940 Hedwig Bercu was registered as a Jew under the terms of the First Order. Clifford Orange annotated her registration form: '*Miss Hedy Bercu has stated that she is an illegitimate child, and that she has never known who her father was – that her mother subsequently married a Roumanian Jew – that her mother was originally Protestant, but adopted her husband's religion.*'

[128] Casper, Remembrances, p.118. The stamps were issued to raise revenue for pensions.

[129] Jersey Evening Post, 11 Oct. 1950

[130] YV, Guernsey papers 0.9; JID, AO file for Hedwig Bercu JB117. In 1938 Clifford Orange incorrectly recorded that Bercu was her father's name and Goldenberg that of her mother. Orange however correctly recorded her parents names when he subsequently registered Bercu as a Jew in October 1940.

Bercu, despite being a Registered Jew, remarkably obtained employment as an interpreter at the transport department of NSKK-Transportgruppe West, Staffel Vt. In this capacity she had access to petrol coupons which she secretly took for distribution to Jersey doctors in order to enable them to have sufficient fuel to visit their sick patients. Bercu was approached by a British lorry driver who demanded that she give him petrol coupons. When she refused he threatened to inform the German authorities.

Realising she was in grave danger Bercu went into hiding on 4 November 1943. She was at first hidden at La Rosiere, Trinity, by Bozena Kotyzova, a Czechoslovakian national previously employed as a housemaid but who now lived alone in the large house. Shortly thereafter, Bercu moved to 7 West Park Avenue in St Helier, the home of Dorothea Weber. Bercu remained in hiding with Mrs Weber until liberation in 1945, during which time she was secretly helped by a German officer who ensured they had sufficient food to survive. Bercu's statement of her efforts to sustain herself includes an account of how she and Dorothea Weber captured a pig at night. They slaughtered the pig in the bathroom of the house and lived on the meat for many days, eating every edible part of the animal. On another occasion in their nighttime search for food they discovered a dead fish on the beach, this they boiled and ate.

In their search for Bercu the Feldkommandant placed a notice together with her photograph in the 'Jersey Evening Post' on 22nd and 23rd of November:

> *'The German authorities are looking for Miss Hedwig Bercu, (see photograph), typist, of no nationality*[131]*, 24 years of age ... She has been missing from her residence since November 4th 1943, and has evaded the German authorities. Any person who knows the whereabouts of Miss Bercu is requested to get in touch with the Feldkommandantur 515, who will treat any information with the strictest confidence. Anyone concealing Miss Bercu or aiding her in any other manner makes himself liable to punishment'.*

On 26 November Heeresjustizinspektor Schroder of the German court-martial Jersey court wrote to Jersey's Attorney General in relation to the '*criminal case against the stateless commercial employee Hedwig Bercu (formerly Goldenberg)*', requiring to be notified if she had any previous convictions. The reply was negative.

---

[131] Bercu may have been re-categorised as a German and stripped of her nationality under the Ordonnance du 2 December 1942 forfeiting the nationality of German Jews living abroad.

Hedwig Bercu's name appears on a '*List of escaped prisoners*' sent by the Platzkommandant to the Bailiff on 15 August 1944 noting: '*Hedwig Bercu (previously Goldenberger) born 23.6.1919 in Vienna, previously interpreter NSKK-Transportgruppe West, Staffel V.*' The German authorities believed that Bercu had escaped to France as a note on her identity card records: '*19 September 1944 – German Police stated Hedy Bercu was in France*'.

The Aliens Office file on Hedwig Bercu notes that she reported to the Aliens Office on 14 May 1945 after the Liberation. Clifford Orange noted in her Aliens Office file '*4.30pm Hedy Bercu reported – stated that she had been living in secret with Mrs Weber [Dorothea Weber, nee Le Brocq] at West Park Avenue, St Helier, for last 18 months, having escaped from the Germans*'.

Bercu remained in Jersey after the war employed at La Ferriere, St Saviour. In January 1947 she made an application to England to take up employment as children's nanny for the Stephens family in Plumpton, Sussex. He objective was to be near the German officer who had helped her in hiding and who had become a British prisoner of war. After his release they married and subsequently lived in Germany. [132]

Dorothea Weber (nee Le Brocq) had married the Austrian born Anton Weber on 26 May 1941. She consequently acquired German nationality and was issued with a new German identity card noting her date of birth as 14 May 1913, St Helier and her occupation as '*household duties*'. The Auslanderlisten notes that Anton Weber was born on 2 August 1913 and that he was employed in Jersey as a baker before joining the Wehrmacht on 15 January 1942. Anton Weber may well have been required to prove his wife's non-Jewish credentials prior to joining the Wehrmacht as Dorothea Weber visited the Feldkommandant to certify that she was not a Jew. The Feldkommandant referred her to the Attorney-General to provide a certificate confirming her non-Jewish status. On 5 January the Attorney-General informed Feldkommandant that as Dorothea Weber was illegitimate he could only provide information as to her mother's family and consequently could not make a definitive statement.

Anton Weber was presumed to have died during the war and on 23 August 1945 Dorothea married Francis Flanagan then serving in the British Army Liberation Forces. [133]

---

[132] JAS, Law Officers File, Sentences and Prosecutions by Field Command Box 20 and B/A/W50/165; JID, AO-Bercu JB117; Author's interviews with Bercu 1998

[133] JID, Auslanderlisten provided by Aliens Office but annotated in German hand; JID, Registration card for Hedwig Bercu; Jersey Registry of Marriages 23 Aug. 1945.

Margarete Hurban, an Austrian and listed as a cook, was married to Hans Hurban a non-Jewish Austrian listed as an houseman. Intriguingly, despite the First Order which prevented Jews who had '*fled the occupied zone*' from returning, the Hurbans travelled from Jersey to Germany on 4 December 1940 returning to the island on 20 December.[134] The Aliens Office General Diary in an entry dated 9 October 1942 records that the Hurbans had not reported their return to the Aliens Office. However Margarete Hurban's German registration card which commences in March 1942 lists that she reported to the German police virtually until February 1945. The Hurbans had a daughter, Helga Margarete born in Jersey on 28 July 1944.

Other residents of Jewish origin during the Occupation

There were a number of other Jews in the Channel Islands who did not register under the First Order but whose fate should be mentioned here.

Suzanne Malherbe and Lucille(y) Schwob, both French nationals, lived at La Rocquaise St, Brelade. Suzanne Malherbe was a renowned surrealist artist under the pseudonym of Marcel Moore and Lucille Schwob established herself as a writer and photographer under the pseudonym of Claude Cahun. From 1941-1944 they distributed a newsletter, '*The Nameless Soldiers*', calling on German soldiers to rise up against their superiors. They were arrested in late 1944 for: '*Unlawful possession of [a] wireless and camera. [and the] Spreading of hostile propaganda with intent to undermine the German Army*'.

After their arrest Malherbe and Schwob both attempted suicide. They were initially sentenced to death by the German Court but this was commuted to life imprisonment after the Bailiff and their advocate appealed to the German authorities for mercy.[135] Baron Von Aufsess, who had succeeded Dr Casper as Chief Administration Officer at the Feldkommandantur, recorded in his published diary that the German authorities believed that they were Jews. Malherbe and Schwob were both released from prison after the Liberation but meanwhile, Lucille

---

[134] JID, Auslanderlisten: Margarete Hurban's German Police registration card does not note that she was a registered Jew listing her German passport as Reisepass Nr 2273 (N); JAS, Law Officers Files

[135] JAS, Law Officers Files, German Field Police Case Files: Malherbe and Schwob were informed on 30 November 1944 of the appeal on their behalf by the Bailiff and Advocate Poch: A senior German officer interviewed in 1990 (Harmsei) stated that the Bailiff had informed the German authorities that 'since time immemorial no woman' had been executed in Jersey. He also stated that in the final months of the war Charles Duret Aubin the Attorney-General had appealed for the release Malherbe and Schwob.

Scwob's health had suffered, she never fully recovered and died in 1954. Malherbe died in Jersey in June 1972.[136]

Connie and Stella Azulay were Jewish half sisters brought up in a London Jewish orphanage. They moved to Jersey with their brother and both later married. Connie Le Marquand and Stella Harvey lived as Methodists throughout the Occupation without being either detected or denounced. In the 1970s they joined the re-established Jersey Jewish Congregation.

David Harris, a carpenter, told the Regal family in the 1960s that he was Jewish and that he had lived in the island during the Occupation without either being detected or denounced.[137]

Dr John Lewis recounted the story of a Jewish patient who went into hiding in 1942. This middle-aged widow had come to Dr Lewis after having received a deportation order, probably under the deportation of non-island born British subjects, in September 1942. Dr Lewis fabricated a medical report seeking her exemption on the grounds of ill-health. When this was rejected she went into hiding with an elderly couple in St Helier, surviving the war undetected.[138]

Three spinster sisters Evelyn, Olive and Nellie Cohen, lived in St Peter Port during the Occupation. They may well have been related to Louis Cohen who evacuated from Guernsey in 1940. Despite their obviously Jewish name and whilst there is no proof that the sisters were Jewish according to the terms of the First Order, there is no indication that they were harassed.

Albert Gustave Bedane hid Mary Erica Richardson for nearly two years from June 1943. Francis Le Sueur, a non-Jew, also hidden by Bedane in 1944 testified '*Mr Bedane not only helped me for two weeks but sheltered a Dutch Jewess for 2 ½ years and he must have known during all that time that he would be shot if caught....The only reason that Mrs Richardson was in hiding was because she was a Jewess*'.[139]
Albert Bedane was born in Angers, France in 1893, arriving in Jersey the following year. He served in the 1/9th Hants Regiment between 1917

---

[136] Jersey Museum Service, notes published on Suzanne Malherbe and Lucille Schwob; Societe Jersiaise, Prisoners box; On the appeal see JAS, Law Officers File, D/Z 30/11/1944 and John Lewis, A Doctor's Occupation (Jersey, 1982), p.203; Baron Von Aufsess, The von Aufsess Diary (London, 1985), p. 61 (entry 28/10/1944); Although it is possible that one of the half-sisters may not have been 'technically' Jewish according to the Nuremberg law, both women are buried in graves marked with 'Stars of David' at St Brelade's parish cemetery.

[137] Author's discussions with Adv. A. Regal April 1997

[138] Lewis, A Doctor's Occupation, pp.47-51.

[139] Jersey Evening Post interview - 1 June 1970; Francis Le Sueur letter to author 23 May 1999; Le Sueur also noted this 'Dutch Jewess' in his book Shadow of the Swastika published in 1990

and 1920 and in the medical staff of the Royal Jersey Militia at the rank of Sergeant. Bedane became a naturalised British subject in Jersey's Royal Court in 1921. By profession he was a Chartered Masseur (physiotherapist) and established a clinic at Greenwood, 45 Roseville Street, St Helier.[140]

Bedane's humanitarianism is well recorded. As well as Francis Le Sueur and Mrs Richardson he hid an escaped French prisoner of war and a number of Russian forced workers. He never sought to derive any material benefit from his humanitarianism and was only able to feed those he was hiding by taking food from his farmer-patients in exchange for his massage services.

Bedane was well aware of the risks involved in hiding escapees. When asked why he had risked his life he testified, *'I had a few nightmares occasionally but I thought that if I was going to be killed I would rather be killed for a sheep than a lamb anyway'*[141]. Notices were regularly published warning islanders that they faced severe penalties if they aided escapees and a number of islanders were deported to concentration camps for aiding escaped forced workers. Typically, Louisa Gould who was denounced for sheltering an escaped forced worker was deported and died in the gas chambers of Ravensbrück.[142]

Mrs Richardson married Edmund Richardson, a sea Captain, born in Lincolnshire, England in 1887. He was not Jewish. From 1933 to 1938 the Richardsons lived at Waverley Place, St Helier, moving to 8 Overseas Flats, Dicq Road, St Saviour before the Occupation.[143] Mrs Richardson, had not registered under the first anti-Jewish Order of October 1940. However in February 1941 she registered under the 'Registration and Identification of Persons (Jersey) Order, 1940' requiring the registration of all islanders for the purposes of issuing identity cards. Although she completed the *'details'* section of the

---

[140] Bedane married Clara Isabel Knowlman (nee Cormiere) of Culmstock, Devon in c1923. Clara was a wealthy widow who had five children by her first husband Harry. She had only one child by Bedane, a daughter, Valerie Mary, born 1925. Clara owned a number of properties in Jersey including Greenwood, Roseville Street where Albert Bedane established his clinic. Before the Occupation Clara and Valerie evacuated from Jersey to Devon where Clara died in 1944. Valerie qualified as a physiotherapist and in 1946 married Graham Macpherson. They emigrated to Australia before returning to High Wycombe, England in c1959. They had four children Duncan, Robin, Susan and Malcolm. Valerie died in 1962/3. Duncan and Robin, Valerie's two eldest children, then lived in Jersey for a time with their grandfather Albert Bedane (who by then resided in St Marks Road, St Helier) before returning to England. (letter from I. Mallet to author 1 June 1999)

[141] Jersey Evening Post interview of Albert Bedane by Jeanne Milne - 1 June 1970;

[142] PRO KV4/78

[143] JEP Almanacs 1933-1939; Bob Sowden showed the author around the apartment at Overseas Flats where the Richardsons lived during the Occupation. In a kitchen cupboard the author found a number of accounts in the name of the Richardsons dating from this period.

registration form as Mary Erica Richardson, she signed the form only as Erica Richardson. It is possible that she only adopted the name 'Mary' at the time of registration. Furthermore she misstated her maiden name as Algenon rather than Olvenich, both probably in an effort to conceal her Jewish origins.

Mrs Richardson completed her 1941 registration form stating her place of birth as '*N. Amsterdam, British Guiana'*, and date of birth as 17 December 1888. However no record of her birth exists in British Guiana.[144] Neighbours remember her as having a Dutch accent and she was described as Dutch by both Albert Bedane and Francis Le Sueur.[145] Her Dutch origins are further suggested by Albert Bedane's statement that Mrs Richardson had written to him after the war promising that he would be recognised by the Dutch government for saving her life. Diane Baguet (nee Sowden) remembered Mrs Richardson as, *'Dutch, quite short in height and of Jewish appearance'*. Patrick Sowden also clearly recalled Mrs Richardson as having a foreign accent.[146] It would seem that this again was an effort to disguise her origins.

On 25 June 1943 Mrs Richardson was '*taken*' by Aliens Office officials to be photographed. The Aliens Office general diary records: '*Mrs Mary Erica Richardson (nee Algernon) of 8, Overseas, Dicq Rd R/C No 30712 taken to Mr Freeman (Scott's) Broad St. -I/D card returned*'. The fact that she was '*taken*' to Scott's the photographers rather than merely required to attend was unusual and it is the only entry of its kind in the Aliens Office diary. A Scott's receipt dated 25 June notes four photographs taken that day. The receipt is signed by Reginald Payne who was the Assistant Registration Officer in charge of affixing photos and it would seem likely that it was either he or the Aliens Office clerk Miss Luxon who escorted Mrs Richardson to Scotts.[147] The photograph attached to her surviving registration card, copies of which were distributed by the Attorney-General on the following day in the search for her, is of studio quality indicating that it was one of those taken at Scotts on 25 June. [148]

---

[144] The Chief Registration Officer, Georgetown, Guyana despite having complete records for births in New Amsterdam, British Guiana has no record of Mary Richardson's birth on or around 17 Dec 1888 (author's enquiry March 1999).

[145] Author's Jan. 1998 and May 1999 interviews with Bob Sowden, and Diane Baguet whose family owned and lived at Overseas Flats

[146] Author's Interview with Patrick Sowden May 1999. Patrick Sowden also confirmed that his family believed she had gone into hiding because she had been uncovered as a Jew

[147] The Aliens Office Diary entry is signed 'E.A.L.' This being the initials of Evelyn Annie Luxon, an Aliens Office clerk; Reginald Payne was appointed in June 1942

[148] Photographs dating from the mass photographing of the general population in 1942 are of inferior quality as they were taken in temporary booths set up for the purpose.

It is probable that Mrs Richardson had not complied with the German Order requiring the mass photographing of the general population in 1942, possibly fearing that her Jewish appearance may alert the German authorities. At the time of the initial registration of the islands population in 1941, due to the lack of photographic materials, photographs were not affixed to the identity cards of British nationals. However in May 1942 all islanders were required to present themselves for photographing at specially established centres in each parish for the purpose of affixing photographs to their personal Identity Card and to each of the two sets of Registration Cards kept by the Aliens Office. In Dec 1942 and May 1943 Clifford Orange, the Chief Registration and Aliens Officer prepared lists of those who had not complied with the photographic order but Mrs Richardson's name does not appear on either list. Those listed were ordered in writing to attend the Aliens Office.[149] Orange wrote to the Attorney-General on 9 March: '*It seems clear, therefore, that these refractory persons can only be compelled to obey the Order by police action, other methods adopted by this Office having failed*'[150]

It is unclear whether Mrs Richardson was '*taken*' to Scotts at the instigation of the Aliens Office or the German authorities, however later that day she went into hiding. Around the time of her attendance at Scotts Mrs Richardson was interviewed by the Germans and ordered for deportation.

The 'Jersey Evening Post' interviewed Albert Bedane in June 1970:

> *'She [Mrs Richardson] had been questioned by the Germans at College House, the Feldkommandantur and was allowed to go home and collect her jewels and valuables because, she was told she was to be sent to a "very nice, special camp where she would be well looked after and she would need her best things with her." While she was getting ready to go to the very nice camp she managed to escape and made her way to Mr Bedane's physiotherapy clinic.'*

Norman Longmate in an account published in 1972 provides a slightly different account of the day's events, apparently derived from a post-war interview with Bedane. He stated that after being interviewed at the Feldkommandantur, Mrs Richardson was escorted home under German guard to pack up her possessions. Mrs Richardson however managed to

[149] Captain Edmund Richardson's registration Card is marked 'Exempted from photographic requirements' on medical grounds.
[150] JAS D/Z 1940/52

divert the attention of her German guard and escaped to Bedane's home.[151]

Whatever the exact circumstances of Mrs Richardson escape, we now know from the Attorney-General's letter to the Constables that she went into hiding at Bedane's clinic on 25 June 1943, the day she was taken to Scotts photographers. Albert Bedane's clinic in Roseville Street was only a few hundred yards from Overseas Flats. The clinic, attached to Bedane's home, incorporated a three roomed cellar of less than five feet in height where Mrs Richardson was at first hidden. After a few months she moved to a net curtained room on an upper floor of the house.[152]

Immediately the Germans realised Mrs Richardson was missing they instigated a search and ordered the Constable of St Helier[153] to inform the other 11 parish Constables of her disappearance. On the following day, 26 June, Jersey's Attorney-General, wrote to the Parish Constables:

> *'I understand that you were recently informed by the Constable of St Helier, in compliance with an Order of the Occupying Authorities, that a Mrs Mary Erica Richardson (nee Algernon) was missing from her last registered address, 8, Overseas Flats, Dicq Road, St Saviour.*
>
> *I have now been requested to forward to you for your information, and to assist you for the purposes of identification, two copies of the photograph of Mrs Richardson which is attached to her registration papers.'*[154]

The Attorney-General annotated his file copy of this letter: *'2.7.43 – Town Hall states that maiden name should read "OLVENICH"'*[155]

One eye-witness well remembers the Germans searching for Mrs Richardson. Patrick Sowden, then eight years of age, was standing outside the block of apartments when two plain-clothed German officers approached in a staff car. They demanded that he direct them to the Richardsons' flat. He led them down the staircase leading to front door

---

[151] Norman Longmate 'If Britain had Fallen', 1972

[152] Whilst the house and clinic have been remodelled and now comprise the Grange Court Hotel, part of the cellars remain. (author viewed the cellars May 1999)

[153] The Constable is the senior elected municipal officer of the parish. There are 12 parishes in Jersey.

[154] Letter from Charles Duret Aubin ,Attorney-General, to the Constable of St Peter, 26 June 1943, Jersey Archive Service - File L/F/54/C/D/22- Occupation Papers of the Constable of St Peter.

[155] JAS D/Z File 1943/16

of No 8 and well remembered his surprise that Captain Richardson feigned senility when questioned by the two German officers.[156]

Bedane recounted, in his 'Jersey Evening Post' interview of June 1970, that whilst in hiding Mrs Richardson changed her hair style, wore dark glasses and occasionally sat out in the garden. She escaped detection by returning to the secret cellar whenever the house was searched by the Germans. In the final weeks of the war Mrs Richardson came out of hiding to care for her husband who was by then an invalid,[157] taking this risk on the assumption that as many of the German forces had been replaced since her disappearance she would have been forgotten. Indeed she survived the remainder of the Occupation without detection.[158]

The 'Jersey Evening Post' noted in their 1970 interview with Bedane: '*Mrs Richardson, before she died, spent some time in an Austrian clinic after the war was over, and she wrote to Mr Bedane from there to thank him again for saving her life, and saying that the Dutch Government would no doubt have been in touch with him.*'

Albert Bedane was presented with a gold watch by the Russian Government in 1965 in recognition of his efforts to save escaped Russian forced workers.[159] However he was never recognised by the Dutch government. Albert Bedane died in Jersey in 1980.

After the details of his heroism emerged an application was made in May 1999 for his posthumous recognition by the State of Israel. This application jointly made by the Holocaust Education Trust and the Jersey Jewish Congregation was endorsed by Prof David Cesarani, Director of the Wiener Library and Lord Jakobovits, the late Chief Rabbi. On 4 January 2000 Yad Vashem announced their formal recognition of Albert Gustave Bedane as '*Righteous among the Nations*', Israel's highest Holocaust honour.

---

156 Interview with Patrick Sowden 21-5-99. Patrick Sowden, now a respected Jersey lawyer was very surprised that Captain Richardson pretended to be senile as he knew very well that he was of sound mind. Members of the Sowden family were told, by their now deceased mother, that when the Germans arrived to search for Mrs Richardson she was bundled into a kitchen cupboard by Captain Richardson. Despite a thorough search she was not discovered. The Sowden family were unaware until long after the war that Mrs Richardson had gone into hiding and had always assumed that she had been deported and had not survived Author's interviews with, Diane Baguet (nee Sowden), Ros Rice (nee Sowden) and Bob Sowden.

157 Mr Terry Sowden QC remembered that Captain Richardson was not an invalid at the beginning of the war and became progressively incapacitated (Discussion with author April 1999)

158 Mrs Richardson's name does not appear on a list of 'escaped prisoners' sent by the Platzkommandant to the Bailiff in August 1944

159 Albert Bedane died in Jersey on 8 Jan 1980. He was cremated at Westmount Crematorium, his ashes were buried at RB 3- R19- P A. By that time an atheist, he requested that no religious service be held. No one attended his funeral.

Finally, Joe Miere, a Jersey Occupation historian, has for many years tried to ascertain the fate of Arthur Samuel Kleinstein and Martha Helga Kleinstein who lived in Midvale Road and ran a shop in Bath Street. The Kleinsteins moved in 1939 to an unknown address. Joe Miere remembers the family as he lived in a neighbouring house. Joe Miere has a photograph of himself with Martha Kleinstein and another of Mr and Mrs Kleinstein walking on the promenade. Joe Miere recalls there was a rumour that the Kleinsteins had drowned in an attempt to escape from Jersey by boat in March 1941. Efforts to uncover any further information on the fate of the Kleinsteins have proved fruitless.

Memorials

The recent chronicling of the fate of the Jews in the Channel Islands during the Occupation has led to the establishment of a number of memorials.

In September 1998 the Jersey Jewish Congregation held a memorial service dedicated to both the Jews who suffered during the Occupation and the non-Jews who came to their aid. The speakers included Sir Philip Bailhache, Bailiff of Jersey; Sir Graham Dorey, Bailiff of Guernsey; Mr Jon Kay-Mouat OBE, President of Alderney; Lord Jakobovits, Emeritus Chief Rabbi; V. Rev. John Seaford, Dean of Jersey; Rev. Malcolm Weisman OBE, Visiting Minister to the Jersey Jewish Congregation.

After the service Lady Jakobovits unveiled a plaque '*Dedicated to the memory of those Jews who suffered during the German occupation of the Channel Islands 1940-1945*'

On 20 July 1999 the Jersey Jewish Congregation held a service in memory of Therese Steiner, Auguste Spitz and Marianne Grunfeld at the new Jewish cemetery in Jersey. After the service a plaque was dedicated

> *'To the memory of Marianne Grunfeld, born Katowice 1912; Auguste Spitz, born Vienna 1901; Therese Steiner, born Vienna 1916; Jewish residents of Guernsey during the German occupation. Deported on 21 April 1942 to their deaths at Auschwitz-Birkenau'*

In February 2000 Sir Philip Bailhache, Bailiff of Jersey, following the United Kingdom government's initiative, announced the establishment of Holocaust Memorial Day in the island as an annual memorial to be held on 27 January, commemorating the day of the liberation of Auschwitz. The programme will include a schools educational effort together with a public memorial event.

In January 2000 the President of the States of Guernsey's Heritage Committee announced the establishment of an official memorial plaque to Steiner, Spitz and Grunfeld to be located at St Peter Port harbour, the place of their deportation from the Island. This plaque is expected to be unveiled on 27 January 2001, Guernsey's first Holocaust Memorial Day.

Summary

This summary aims to highlight important elements of the chronicle of the wartime anti-Jewish Orders and to place them within the context of post-war memories and the investigations carried out after the war.

Many of the documents of the civilian authorities and the German occupiers relating to the anti-Jewish measures in the islands have been lost or were destroyed. However what has survived represents a staggering quantity of administrative paperwork considering it concerns so few individuals. Furthermore it vividly illustrates the importance the Germans placed upon rooting out and discriminating against the few Jews even in the Channel Islands.

The Channel Islands were the only part of Great Britain to fall under German occupation. Significantly the anti-Jewish Orders in Jersey, Guernsey and Sark were enforced in the islands not by the SS or special anti-Jewish units but by, and under the direction of the ordinary offices of the administrative arm of German army.

The preparatory measures referred to in Colonel Knackfuss's letter of 23 January 1942 for the removal of the mentally inferior to institutions, albeit that for reasons of Hitler's change of policy the measure may not have been implemented, indicates that other genocidal elements of Nazi ideology were also planned for these 'British' islands.

In July 1940 the Island authorities had little choice, if they wished to retain their offices, other than to accept the German proclamation:

> *'The Orders of the German Commandant heretofore now and hereafter issued shall in due course be registered in the records of the Island of Jersey, in order that no person may plead ignorance thereof'.*

Bailiff Coutanche regarded this proclamation as having been *'of supreme importance'* in defining the relationship with the German administration.[160] A direct consequence of this proclamation was the decision to register the first anti-Jewish Order in the islands' Royal Courts in October 1940 and the subsequent orders were registered

[160] H.R.S. Pocock, The Memoirs of Lord Coutanche, p.21

following this precedent. Although the authorities had ample evidence that the anti-Jewish orders were cumulatively significantly affecting the lives of the registered Jews it was only when the Eight Order was presented to Bailiff Coutanche that he and Attorney-General Aubin seemingly re-examined the moral and legal issues. The evidence indicates a successful appeal to the German administrators against the registration of the Order. There is however no evidence that any further protests were made against the anti-Jewish orders and in Guernsey even the Eighth order appears to have been registered without objection.

The promulgation in the Royal Courts provided local endorsement to the first anti-Jewish Order and undoubtedly contributed to island residents compliance with its registration requirements. Registration simply being the process of law abiding citizens complying with the law of the Royal Courts.[161] Not registering posed too great a risk for some island residents who were already known to the authorities or listed as resident aliens. Some had arrived in the islands as refugees of persecution in Europe and become trapped by the Occupation. Three who registered in Jersey were descendants of long established Jewish families and may have considered that their Jewish origins were known. Those who registered did not foresee the ultimate effects of their actions as is unequivocally illustrated by Esther Lloyd's diary entry of May 1943, written at Biberach, *'Never shall I be honest again - if I had not declared myself this wouldn't have happened'*.[162]

There was only one recorded objection to the registration of the first anti-Jewish Order. Ambrose Sherwill, the Attorney-General of Guernsey, in his unpublished memoirs, recounted the objection made by Sir Abraham Laine, a Jurat of Guernsey's Royal Court:

> *'I noted its provisions [from the German command in Paris] which included the required wearing by all Jews of the yellow star of David. It disgusted me and I visualised Jews being jeered at on Guernsey in the streets, pelted with filth and generally harassed, but I had no premonition of the appalling atrocities which were to be perpetrated on them by the Nazi regime.*
>
> *I made such enquiries as I could and learned, accurately as it turned out, that the few Jews who had settled on Guernsey had all evacuated. In these circumstances, I felt no purpose would*

[161] As a comparison even Jersey's Attorney-General felt that he had an obligation to pass on police reports to the German authorities according to the terms of the 'Order for the protection of the Occupying Authority' when this 'became the law of the Island'. (see Attorney-General's memorandum 4 Aug 1945, JAS D/Z Law Officers files)

[162] Esther Pauline Lloyd diaries 6 May 1943, The Wiener Library

> *be served in ... advising the Royal Court to refuse to register it. If I had, presumably the Germans would have threatened the Royal Court by marching in armed soldiers.*
>
> *Nevertheless, I still feel shamed that I did not do something by way of protest to the Germans: a vital principle was at stake even if no human being in Guernsey was actually affected. The honour of refusing to concur in registration fell to Sir Abraham Laine who, when called on as a Jurat to vote on the matter, openly and categorically refused his assent and stated his grave objections to such a measure'.*[163]

However no mention of Laine's objection is contained in any of the British Intelligence reports prepared in the early post liberation period (see below) and Laine is listed as one of the Jurats participant in the promulgation of the First Order in the Royal Court of Guernsey on 23 October 1940.

Ralph Durand in an account, published in 1946, of the circumstances surrounding the registration of the First Order also makes no reference to Laine's objection

> *'It seems more probable that each member of the Royal Court present at the special sitting considered that to refuse his vote for the registration of the order, however much it offended his conscience and judgement would be futile........*
>
> *It is the duty of a jurat....to vote against the registration of any order of which he does not approve. Since it seems incredible that the jurats concerned approved the "Measures against the Jews" Order it surely follows that they voted for its registration because they had no choice in the matter. In other words the German authorities imposed their will on the Royal Court'*[164]

We know that Sherwill as Attorney-General was aware that four Jews were registered in Guernsey and had not all evacuated as he claimed and even Durand was aware that '*half a dozen people were affected by the Measures against Jews*'. Sherwill's account also confuses the terms of the First and Eighth orders. A possible explanation for the lack of other accounts of Laine's objection was that he may have felt honour-bound not to reveal the private deliberations of Guernsey's Jurats and therefore did not disclose the facts either publicly or to British Intelligence. Although there is no suggestion that Sir Abraham Laine's objection did

---

[163] Cruickshank, The German Occupation, p.113; The Rev Douglas Ord also initially presumed that all the Jewish residents of Guernsey had left the island before the war, noting in his diary on 24 Oct. 1940 'Thank God the few we had are safely in England'.

[164] Ralph Durand, 'Guernsey Under German Rule', Guernsey 1946

not occur, it is regrettable that Sherwill's brief reference, in his otherwise deficient account, remains the sole source on this principled objection.

Despite the uncertainty surrounding the exact details of Sir Abraham Laine's objection other acts of objection are well documented. Bailiff Coutanche and Attorney-General Aubin's intervention in relation to the Eighth Order in 1942 was a significant act of principle. It was motivated solely by humanitarian considerations, as it took place at a time when the German forces were winning the war on all fronts and the end of the Occupation could not realistically have been foreseen. In November 1944 Bailiff Coutanche pleaded for mercy in the case against Suzanne Malherbe and Lucille Schwob, a course also taken by their lawyer Advocate Giffard and their actions probably saved their lives.[165]

Documentary evidence also shows that some legal administrators of absentee Jews, whilst having initially made declarations regarding their clients identity and assets, subsequently endeavoured to ensure that these assets were protected. In the case of Catherine Hill, her lawyer Mr Poch protested that his absentee client had been categorised as a Jew. Poch evidently went to considerable lengths to prove his point. His assertion that she was of advanced years and needed the income emphasises his commitment as clearly funds could not be remitted to her in England whilst the island was still under Occupation.

Documentary evidence also details the individual acts, at great personal risk, of Dorothea Weber who hid Hedwig Bercu for over 18 months and of Albert Bedane who hid Mrs Richardson for nearly two years.

In much of occupied Europe the Germans were able to rely upon viciously antisemitic locals to implement their measures against the Jews. This co-operation by local civilians and military officers ranged from administrative assistance to arranging transportations to death camps and active participation in the mass murder of Jews. The background in Jersey, Guernsey and Sark was fundamentally different. In the absence of a background of centuries of extreme antisemitic feeling towards the islands small Jewish population the Germans had little to focus upon and amplify. Although the authorities in Jersey and Guernsey registered and implemented the German anti-Jewish measures they did not do this within the context of venting centuries of antisemitism as was the case in many other Occupied areas.

The Germans went to considerable effort to influence islanders with Nazi antisemitic propaganda, evidenced by the proliferation of anti-Jewish articles in the local press. The film *Jew Suss* was specially adapted for a

[165] Advocate Giffard had been imprisoned for 2 months for insulting the German authorities in 1940.

British audience by the addition of English subtitles when shown in Jersey and Guernsey. Even the public recital of music by Jewish composers was censored and Mendelssohn could only be played in Guernsey in September 1943 on condition that his name was not advertised. The Feldkommandantur also monitored the books available for sale locally both to islanders and to the German troops, destroying copies of *Der Abenteurer* after they deemed that part of the text deviated from Nazi ideological views on Jews.[166]

Despite these attempts to stimulate antisemitism, there is little evidence that islanders were spurred into denouncing suspected Jews. The complex case of Julia Brichta is the only documented case of a denunciation of a supposedly Jewish Guernsey resident. Similarly a letter sent to the Feldkommandantur in 1943 and subsequently passed on to the Bailiff is the only evidence of a Jersey resident having invoked the language of Nazi antisemitism into the area of general denunciations. The anonymous author of this letter in denunciation of a suspected black-marketeer wrote: '*is this man English-man or Jew?*'[167] Although there were post-war suggestions that Marianne Grunfeld was exposed by a fellow worker and we are unsure as to exactly how Mrs Richardson was uncovered there is no documentary evidence indicating that either was denounced.

Before the Occupation, Jersey leaders had been aware of the dangers a Nazi occupation posed to the island's Jewish residents and had encouraged known Jews to evacuate from the island, the Krichefski family having been advised to leave by the Constable of St Helier. Some islanders had even endeavoured to divest themselves of obvious Jewish associations evidenced by the painting out of the sign over the shop 'P. Moses' in St Helier.[168]

In Guernsey, other than Sir Abraham Laine's protest, there was no further significant documented opposition on the part of the island authorities to the anti-Jewish measures. The Guernsey authorities did not offer substantial documented opposition to the deportation of Steiner, Spitz and Grunfeld in April 1942, albeit that the authorities were most unlikely to have known that the deportees would ultimately perish. The

---

[166] The decision of the Guernsey censor Schmidt-Walkov: Rev. Ord Sept. 1943; Mendelssohn's father had in fact converted to Christianity; Longmate, If Britain Had Fallen, p.149; Falla, The Silent War, p.32; Cruickshank, The German Occupation, p.170.

[167] JAS D/Z Law Officers Files . Letter received by the Feldkommandantur 8 Sept 43 and passed on to the Bailiff on the following day

[168] The Constable of St Helier is the elected head of that Parish equivalent to mayor; Authors interview with Vera Braynis 1998; Jersey Occupation Remembered, Sonia Hillsdon, 1986, p 115; The Jersey Evening Post Almanac 1939 lists 'Moses. P. (Branch) No 6 La Motte Street, St Helier.

Guernsey civilian police informed some of the Jews of their imminent deportation but they were not required to escort them to the port of embarkation. The only documented evidence of an appeal against this deportation is the letter of introduction to the Feldkommandantur provided to Edward Ogier by John Leale the, President of the Controlling Committee. Two months later the Guernsey authorities registered the degrading 'Yellow Star' Order without protest and the Bailiff ordered the Greffier to send translations of the Order to the two remaining Jewish residents. The order was even registered in Sark after Guernsey's Bailiff sent a copy of the Order to the Greffier of Sark.[169]

In Jersey the island authorities similarly provided the Germans with the bureaucratic mechanism enabling the implementation of the discriminatory Orders against the Jews. The Bailiff specifically delegated the matter of registration of Jewish individuals and businesses to Clifford Orange. Orange managed the declarations and day-to-day administration but he carried out the requisite inquiries ultimately under the authority of his superiors, the Bailiff and Attorney-General. The implementation of the anti-Jewish measures was largely carried out in an insensitive bureaucratic manner but comparison with Orange's implementation of the all-island 'Registration and Identification of Persons Order of 1940' indicates that he was similarly rigorous in its enforcement. What is clear is that Orange did not differentiate between those who were in breach of the general all-island registration orders and Jews who were obviously being singled out for persecution solely on the basis of their grandparents religion. Furthermore Orange specifically advised administrating lawyers and accountants of their absolute obligation to register absent Jews and Jewish business interests. The Attorney-General however ultimately dealt with the *Aryanization* of Jewish businesses, a measure affecting both resident and evacuated Jews.

Clifford Orange required a number of individuals to complete Jewish registration forms under the First Order of 1940 who did not strictly fit the definition of a Jew as specified in the German order. The order required that the civilian authorities register only those with more than two Jewish grandparents or who had belonged to the Jewish religion. Davidson had informed Orange that only one of his grandparents was to his knowledge a Jew and Bercu had no blood Jewish grandparents. Orange did not have conclusive evidence that either '*had belonged*' to the Jewish religion. Furthermore, Hyam Goldman was the only Jersey declarant who listed his present religion as '*Judaism*', all the others

[169] The first nine Orders against the Jews were all registered in Sark, sent to the Seneschal by the Guernsey Greffier on the instructions of Guernsey's Bailiff

either declared themselves presently to be Christians or stated that they had no religion.

Except in the case of Marianne Blampied, all the registration forms were completed by Orange himself, and then signed by the individual declarant. In the cases of Davidson, Jacobs and Bercu, Orange annotated the registration forms with sufficient information to have enabled the declarants' exclusion from classification as Jews under the terms of the order. Hurban, then a Roman Catholic, could also have been excluded had Orange not completed her form listing her as *'originally Jewish'*. Only Esther Lloyd's form states *'Both Mrs Lloyd's parents are Jews'*.

Orange wrote to the Bailiff on 25 October 1940 enclosing, *'copies, in triplicate, of the completed forms'*. Clearly the Bailiff and Attorney-General were aware of the line taken by their delegated subordinate, Orange and there was sufficient doubt based on the information supplied on the registration forms to have at the very least stimulated further inquiries before all twelve were included on the list of registered Jews passed on to the Germans. Had such inquiry taken place it is most doubtful that Bercu, as but one example, would have been categorised as a Jew. Undoubtedly a sympathetic interpretation of the definitions of the First Order would have allowed the exclusion of a number of those subsequently listed as registered Jews.[170]

Esther Lloyd after her repatriation and significantly whilst the islands were still under German occupation, protested to Bailiff Coutanche. In her letter of September 1944 Lloyd stated that she had informed Clifford Orange that she *'was catholic on my mother's side......I went to register at the Aliens Office at the time an order was brought out concerning Jews as I am of Jewish origin on my Grandfather's side only, I thought at the time it concerned me but if all the facts concerning myself had been fully explained to the German authorities, there would have been no question of my being sent away'*. Lloyd demanded to know *'why these facts have been suppressed and wish the matter gone into'*.[171]

Clifford Orange in his written explanation to the Bailiff stated: *'In each case of registration, [under the First Order] the person concerned was told by me that the responsibility for registering or not registering under the Order rested entirely with the individual concerned, and Mrs Lloyd was informed accordingly'*. This statement does not reflect the weight of evidence to the contrary. Furthermore Esther Lloyd's appeal and diary

---

170 Island of Jersey, AO, Orders relating to measures against Jews, GEN/3/1940.

171 Orange has made no mention of Esther Lloyd's claim to have stated that she had Catholic ancestors on her registration form of Oct 1940. Orange has annotated the form 'both Mrs Lloyd's parents are Jews'

entries show that this was not her recollection of Orange's handling of the registration process. Bercu similarly did not recall having been offered any choice by Orange as to whether or not she should register.[172]

At the very same time that declarations under the first anti-Jewish Order were being prepared by Orange and passed on to the Germans by his superiors, other declarations were being sought by the Attorney-General in respect of '*members of the British Armed Forces in hiding in Jersey*'. In July 1940 under the Orders of the Feldkommandant serving members of the British Armed Forces had been required to declare themselves. On 23 October the Feldkommandant instructed the Attorney-General to seek declarations from '*all members of the British Armed Forces in hiding in Jersey, or any persons assisting them in any way*'. The following day the Feldkommandant placed a notice in the 'Jersey Evening Post' stating: '*Members of the British Armed Forces obeying this Order will be treated as prisoners of war and no measures will be taken against persons who have assisted them*'. Declarations were to be made within two days. The Attorney-General then supplied a summary list of the seven declarants to the Feldkommandant. However in an effort to limit any discriminatory effects resulting from the declarations the Attorney-General carefully detailed any facts in each declarants favour. In consequence, on 25 November the Feldkommandant informed the Bailiff :

> '*Of the seven persons reported in the letter of 26 October 1940 from the Attorney General, only one .... is to be considered as an active member of the British Armed Forces. He is, therefore, a prisoner of war. His transportation to a prison camp cannot be considered at present on account of his health*'.[173]

We can only speculate at the likely outcome had the declarations under the First Order against the Jews been accompanied by similar mitigating evidence detailing the areas of doubt as to the applicability of the order to each declarant.

Clifford Orange further demonstrated a tendency towards over-inclusiveness in his examination of the Register of Limited Liability Copies in 1941. Orange in his hand written file notes recorded '*qy (sic) David Dumosch Ltd ?*'. Although the founder of this company was a Dutch Jew, the then owners were not practising Jews and the name

[172] Island of Jersey, AO, Orders relating to measures against Jews, GEN/3/1940. Letter from Clifford Orange to the Bailiff 23 September 1944

[173] JAS Law Officers Files D/Z: The declarant was resident at St saviour's Mental Institution and was 'a certified patient of unsound mind'

Dumosch would hardly have been regarded by the Germans as Jewish.[174] Similarly, Orange's file notes identifying island residents William Harry Leopold and Alfred Ephraums as possible Jews, put them at potential risk as they had not made declarations under the First Order particularly as we know that the file was inspected by the Germans in January 1942.

The civilian authorities were aware throughout the Occupation of the German agenda to root-out any undeclared Jews. On 5 February 1942 the Bailiff was notified by the Feldkommandant: '*It is to be ascertained at once and I am to be informed as to whether a British subject Ramon Alfred Gordon, resident in St Brelade is a Jew or not*'. The Attorney-General wrote to the Constable of St Brelade for further information. On 17 February Dr Reffler demanded an immediate response and on 21 February the Attorney-General replied that Gordon had '*left the island before the occupation... and they do not know, nor have they been able to discover, anything about him which would enable them to say whether he is or is not a Jew.*'[175]

The Aliens Office involvement in '*taking*' Mrs Richardson to be photographed and the Attorney-General's subsequent letter notifying the Constables all took place in June 1943, four months after the civilian authorities had certain knowledge of the special risk of deportation facing Jews.

In February 1943 Jersey's Royal Court passed the 'Order for the protection of the Occupying Authority'. This order formalised the obligation of '*the local Law Officers*' to pass on and assist the Germans in cases involving of infractions of German occupation legislation. In consequence the Attorney-General considered that this Order imposed a legal obligation upon him to assist the Germans in their efforts to apprehend those who were in contravention of Occupation law even if their offence was only against the German regime.[176]

Despite the Attorney-General's seemingly rigid interpretation of his obligations under the law, and his file note regarding Mrs Richardson's maiden name, his letter to the Constables in relation her disappearance is very carefully worded. He stops short of ordering the instigation of a search for her, alternatively enclosing photographs to be used for '*the*

---

[174] David Dumosch Limited, a firm of potato merchants, was founded by a Dutch Jew in 1925. The founder (David snr) died in the 1930's and by the outbreak of war the business was run by his son David jnr. There is no evidence that David snr's wife was a Jew and therefore no presumption that David jnr would have been regarded as a Jew under the terms of the First Order.

[175] JAS file D/Z 1940/49 Jewish Undertakings etc

[176] 'Order for the protection of the Occupying Authority' registered in Jersey's Royal Court 13 Feb 1943

purposes of identification'. Furthermore there is no evidence to suggest that the Jersey Police actively searched for Mrs Richardson and in 1944 the Feldkommandantur protested to the Bailiff that the Police were not providing the required level of co-operation as Jersey police officers were not '*energetically*' implementing German orders to search for missing persons.[177]

The final stages of the *Aryanization* of Jewish business program in Jersey were implemented by Attorney-General Aubin under direct instructions of the Feldkommandant. By far the most tragic case was that of the closing of Nathan Davidson's small grocery business and there is no documentary evidence to indicate that any appeal was made to help Davidson. Mrs Goldman's successful appeal was only as a result of her protest to the Feldkommandantur. The correspondence in the Law Officer's file 'Jewish Undertakings Etc' presents a distressing account of this episode compounded by our knowledge of Davidson's fall to poverty, his breakdown and ultimately his premature death at St Saviour's Mental institution.

The appeals by Mrs Goldman and by Mr Poch on behalf of Mrs Hill, illustrate that the German authorities in Jersey were, at least for a time, prepared to listen to reasoned legal argument in relation to the strict interpretation of who should be categorised as a Jew under the First Order. This has obvious relevance when considering which of the twelve registered Jews would have been required to be listed in October 1940 had reasoned argument been put before the Germans. Notably, it was not until the Third Order in June 1941 that a presumption was included that in '*doubtful*' cases an individual '*shall be deemed to be a Jew*'.

The deportation of Steiner, Spitz and Grunfeld from Guernsey in April 1942 occurred very early in the chronology of the implementation of the Final Solution in the western zone of occupied Europe. The deportation, initially to Laval, represented the first stage of a journey that ultimately led to their deaths at Auschwitz-Birkenau. It was not exclusively a deportation of Jews and Millicent McGahy, an American non-Jew, was included in the transportation but only McGahy was not sent on to an extermination camp.

In April 1942, the nationality of the island's Jews provided the key to deportation, as illustrated by the treatment of Steiner and Spitz as compared to their co-Austrian/German national, Elisabet Duquemin. The British nationality Duquemin had acquired through marriage

[177] JAS file B/A/W50/165 Letter from Platzkommandant Major Heider to Bailiff of Jersey 15 Aug 1944

offered her protection from deportation; Elda Brouard was similarly protected.

None of the Jews who had registered in Jersey were deported in April 1942. The Jews of British nationality were protected at that time in the same way as their co-nationals in Guernsey. The one Egyptian national may have been similarly protected from deportation as an Order dated February 1942 stated that Egyptian subjects were to be considered as nationals of the British Empire.[178] The deportation of Romanian nationals from Jersey would also have been questionable as the matter of the deportation of Romanian exile Jews had not yet been resolved by Berlin.[179] Margarete Hurban, the one German national, may have been temporarily protected as she was married to a German national who was not Jewish. Wranowsky in Sark as a German national was probably only spared as she had appealed against having been classified as a Jew.

Dr Casper's request, in June 1942, for clarification from his superiors in Paris on the question of whether or not the 'Jewish Star' Order applied to British Jews, further reinforces the significance of nationality at that time. Despite the Bailiff of Guernsey ordering that the two remaining Jews in the island should be notified of the terms of the Eighth Order and Dr Brosch ordering supplies of Jewish stars, no formal decision appears to have been received from Paris as to the application of the Order to British Jews.

The deportation of Jews as one of the specific categories in February 1943 was subsequent to the general deportation of non-indigenous British subjects from the islands in September 1942, a measure against which the island civilian authorities had offered documented objection. We know that the Jersey authorities were aware at least seven days before the deportation of 13 February 1943 of the identity of the majority of those who were scheduled for deportation. Applications by a few departments of the States of Jersey and Guernsey for exemptions on behalf of small number of essential employees were granted by the Germans. As an example, the Jersey Police authorities obtained exemption for Albert Chardinc, originally on the list for having committed an act of resistance against the German regime. Other exemptions from deportation were granted as a result of direct application by the intended deportee to the Feldkommandantur in Jersey and Guernsey rather than through any official representation on the part

[178] GAS, File FK 13-1, Order concerning Enemy Property in the Channel Islands, 20 Feb 1942.

[179] As part of the Axis alliance, the agreement between Berlin and the Romanian government on the question of the deportation of Romanian national Jews living outside Romania had not yet been resolved. See Hilberg, The Destruction of the European Jews, p. 783.

of the civilian authorities and no documented official appeal was made on behalf of the Jews.

The deportation of February 1943 was initially to internment camps rather than concentration camps. Jews were a primary designated category for this deportation and their nationality was no longer the principle issue in the matter of selection. However, with the exception of John Finkelstein, the other Jewish deportees in February 1943 were British nationals, either by birth or marriage. Although as the deportation documents reveal they were selected only because they were Jews, after their deportation British nationality still offered some protection, ensuring that they were not sent on to concentration camps and not separated from the other Channel Island deportees. Only John Max Finkelstein as a Romanian was not protected by nationality and he was transferred from Laufen internment camp to Buchenwald concentration camp and from there, in the final days of the war, to Theresienstadt.

John Finkelstein survived Buchenwald and Theresienstadt. The remaining Jewish deportees and their families together with the other Channel Island internees were liberated from Biberach and Liebenau internment camps in April 1945.

Although all the known Jews were deported from Guernsey not all those registered in Jersey met the same fate. As was the case in many parts of occupied Europe the German mechanism for deportation to both internment and death camps was dependent to some extent on the priorities of the officials in charge of matters concerning Jews at local level.

In Jersey the implementation of measures against the Jews seems to have only been fully understood by those closely involved in the measures including, Bailiff Coutanche, Attorney-General Aubin and Aliens Officer Orange. Even members of Jersey's Superior Council do not appear to have been aware of the extent or effect of the measures. The recently published diary of Edward Le Quesne, a member of Jersey's Superior Council, contains only a few entries relating to resident Jews. Le Quesne noted: *'19 October 1940 - All Jews must be registered and their ancestry investigated for three generations back. Fortunately the number of Jews in Jersey is small'*. The only other significant entries of February 1943 show only that Le Quesne was aware that Jews had been specifically included in the deportations.

Although the general population were aware of the registration of the anti-Jewish orders as many had been published in local newspapers, most islanders do not seem to have fully understood their effect on the small number of resident Jews. Furthermore most islanders do not appear to have been aware that Jews had been specifically selected for inclusion in the deportation of specific categories in February 1943, the issue being confused with the general deportation of mainland born British subjects in September 1942. Only one national newspaper raised the issues of the registration of the anti-Jewish orders and the deportations.[180]

After the Liberation there was an investigation into the measures that had been imposed against the islands' Jews. However the reports compiled by British Military Intelligence and the public statements of the British government require some examination as they provide a complex dichotomy.

A general movement demanding constitutional reform of the islands system of government emerged after Liberation. By August 1945 the atmosphere had become quite heated, British Intelligence reporting:

> *'Colonel Cussen is aware of the rather active political rumblings which are making themselves felt in the Channel Islands and the Director of Public Prosecutions is in touch with the Home Secretary on the question of possible action for the reformation of the Islands' Constitution. We all feel that something will certainly have to be done as otherwise serious trouble may develop. So strong is this feeling that the Force Commander told me the other day that he is afraid armed disturbances may take place when he withdraws his Forces'*[181]

In this atmosphere of discontent a group of Jerseymen raised a petition to the King listing, as one of many points, the civilian authorities registration of the anti-Jewish Orders. On 18 June 1945 the Home Secretary wrote to the Bailiff of Jersey detailing the variety of complaints '*made about the conduct of the island's administration during the recent occupation*'. Bailiff Coutanche submitted a twenty five page detailed response, noting in relation to the criticism of the registration of the anti-Jewish Orders:

> *'The Court had no option but to register this German Order. There was no consternation. The number of persons affected was extremely small and moderation was shown in the execution of the Order.*

[180] See generally 'The personal diary of Deputy Edward Le Quesne; The Daily Worker July 1945.

[181] Substantial constitutional reform of the islands democratic system of government was implemented in the post war period; PRO KV4/78

> *It could be shown that other oppressive measures against the Jews were entirely avoided by proper intervention by the Insular Authorities.'*

The investigations by British Military Intelligence resulted in a number of reports being submitted to Whitehall. One Intelligence report dated 17 August 1945 concluded:

> '*When the Germans proposed to put their anti-Jewish measures into force, no protest whatever was raised by any of the Guernsey Officials, and they hastened to give the Germans every assistance. By contrast, when it was proposed to take steps against the Freemasons, of which there are many in Guernsey, the Bailiff made considerable protests and did everything possible to protect the Masons'.*
>
> *.... In Jersey the attitude of the States and of the Bailiff, Alexander Moncrieff Coutanche does not seem to have quite so gratuitously friendly as it was in Guernsey, but was still very far from being satisfactory'* [182]

This reference to Bailiff Carey's efforts to '*protect the Masons*' requires some explanation. In November 1941 the Germans had proposed that the civilian authorities implement measures to ensure '*the liquidation of Masonic Lodges and their assets*'. The Bailiffs of Jersey and Guernsey sought to ensure that the civilian authorities should not be seen to be openly associated with the proposed measures. On 24 November 1941 Alexander Coutanche wrote to Victor Carey with regard to the German order to confiscate Masonic property:

> '*We have urged that whatever has to be done, should be done by German Order and not by local legislation. I have this morning seen ...[leading Jersey Freemasons] in consultation with Duret Aubin, and they have left me to endeavour to work out a scheme for a voluntary transfer of assets to the States. I have reason to think that some such scheme may be acceptable to all concerned.*'[183]

The Bailiff's refusal to be directly involved in the confiscation of Masonic property may have had one indirect benefit in relation to the implementation of the anti-Jewish measures. It may explain why, in February 1942, Dr Reffler the head of the Feldkommandantur's Financial Affairs department, ordered that the civilian authorities must

---

[182] PRO HO 45/22399 Intelligence Report dated 17 Aug 1945

[183] Jersey Archive Service B/A/W30/13 Letter from the Bailiff of Guernsey to the Bailiff of Jersey 21 Nov 1941 and reply 24 Nov 1941

not be involved in the possible requisitioning of houses belonging to Jews. Furthermore any transfer of the freehold interest of Jewish owned property, a measure carried out in many other parts of Occupied Europe, would have required that the Germans involve the civilian authorities. Island civil law would have required that formal contracts be passed through the Royal Courts.

Despite the critical British Military Intelligence report cited above, the political line from the start had been largely supportive of the civilian authorities. The government took a more pragmatic approach to the actions of the islands civilian administration in the realisation that they had little alternative other than to co-operate to some extent with German orders. Furthermore the government undoubtedly realised that fruitless criticism of the administration would only fuel the rumbling political unrest.

In parliamentary questions to the Secretary of State for the Home Department the following draft was prepared:

> *'Mr Coutanche said that they were bound in general to register the orders of the military authorities otherwise the Germans would have governed by direct action. He understood that some question had been raised as regards registering certain orders with regard to Jews. As regards that, they had registered two orders which could be administered in such a way that they did no harm, all money and securities having been sent out of the country. They absolutely refused to register an order requiring Jews to wear a special badge. He thought it would have been hopeless to take up the line with the Germans that they would have nothing to do with anti-Jewish measures...*
>
> *Mr Aubin [Attorney-General] said that so far from the Jews themselves feeling that they had been badly treated by the local administration, he had since the liberation been thanked by a prominent member of the Jewish community.'*[184]

This statement is however curious, suggesting that the British government was only aware of the registration of the first two orders against the Jews. The claim that the orders *'did no harm'* further emphasises the government's lack of awareness that a dozen orders had been implemented with significant effects. The remark attributed to the Attorney-General could not have been made by any of the resident registered Jews, as not one of the survivors could possibly have been described as *'a prominent member of the Jewish community'*. The

[184] PRO 11046/25844

statement was likely made by one of the Jews who had evacuated and whose business had been protected by a straw-man sale. This government statement seems to have marked the end of the investigation into the implementation of the anti-Jewish measures.

Just after Liberation, the Director of Public Prosecutions had visited Jersey and Guernsey for four days interviewing '*the Military Commander and members of his staff, the security officers, the Bailiffs, Attorneys-General and other members of the Islands' administration.*' His report to the Under Secretary of State for Home Affairs of 9 July 1945 concluded in relation to the conduct of the Guernsey administration; '*there is no prima facie case for suggesting that the administration was in any sense disloyal.*' In relation to the Jersey administration, he concluded '*there are no grounds for suggesting that the administration was disloyal or collaborationist, but all the evidence that I have seen goes to show that the Bailiff and Attorney-General... were remarkably successful in securing every possible advantage for the Islanders*'. The Director of Public Prosecutions accepted that '*the administration made mistakes*' but these had been as a direct consequence of the compromises necessitated by a Nazi occupation. [185]

Another aspect of British Military Intelligence's investigations concerned the activities of the few island collaborators. Initially the British government considered prosecutions where strong evidence was available and a number were interviewed by Military Intelligence. The Director of Public Prosecutions initially concluding: '*we should certainly consider taking action in a limited number of cases*'.[186] However enthusiasm waned when the government realised the legislative and evidential difficulty of guaranteeing successful prosecutions.

There was similarly little enthusiasm to instigate prosecutions against members of the German forces in the islands. The Director of Public Prosecutions had concluded: '*taking the Occupation as a whole the Germans appear to have behaved comparatively well*'. Attorney-General Aubin provided descriptions of Colonel Knackfuss, Dr Brosch and Baron von Aufsess to British Military Intelligence.[187] It would seem that their actions in relation to the implementation of the anti-Jewish policies were never fully investigated. Dr Casper had left the islands in November 1943 for Denmark and again although he had been directly involved in the deportation of Jews from Jersey and Guernsey no prosecution was ever mounted.

---

[185] PRO HO 45/ 22399

[186] PRO KV4/78

[187] DPP report 9 July 1945; JAS Law Officers Files D/Z descriptions of German officers handed to British Military Intelligence by the Attorney-General 9 Aug 1945

Dr Casper had seemingly maintained a cordial working relationship with the civilian authorities. Superior Council member Edward Le Quesne noted in his diary *'10 November 1943 – Lt Casper ...was the most respected and most helpful of all the German officers stationed in Jersey'*. Attorney-General Aubin wrote to Dr Casper in 1963:

> *'I often think of the days when our respective duties brought us into contact, and remember with gratitude the courtesy and consideration you always showed me in very difficult circumstances'*[188]

Alexander Coutanche rarely commented on the fate of the islands Jews during the Occupation and when interviewed in the 1970's recollected

> *'The Jews were I think, called upon to declare themselves. Some did, some didn't ... Those that didn't weren't discovered. I've never heard that they suffered in any way.'*[189]

Clifford Orange seemingly reproached himself in relation to the anti-Jewish measures when shortly after the war, by chance, he met Hedwig Bercu in St Helier. He embraced her and expressed his relief that she had survived. He apologised for his actions stating *'I had to follow German orders'*.[190]

The island authorities had sought to respond to the extraordinarily pressures and moral dilemmas presented by an enemy occupation. Their

---

188 Dr Casper in correspondence with various parties made a number of curious, contradictory and unsubstantiated claims. In an interview conducted in 1990 Casper stated 'If they [the Jersey authorities] had refused [to co-operate generally with the German occupying authorities] the SS Police would have come to the Islands. Neither the Military Government not the Military Commander ..., wanted this and saw to it that things went as smoothly as possible so that having the SS police could be avoided'.

In 1992 Casper claimed 'the notification of those concerned [the Jewish deportees of 13 February 1943] and the transport to the ships was carried out by the Island government to avoid the involvement of the SS Police'. Casper then went on to claim that he had instructed the Attorney-General to offer the Jewish deportees the opportunity of escaping to England but they had refused because of the strong tides in the English Channel.

In 1997 Casper claimed 'When the Order for deportation of the Jews arrived I told General Von Schmettow that the deportation was contrary to international law and asked him therefore to distract the coastguards'. In 1999 Casper again claimed that he had wanted to give the Jews 'the opportunity to sail to England unhindered by Germans'. He stated that he had informed Duret Aubin and instructed Prince Oettingen to inform Bailiff Carey in Guernsey that the 'navy and the coast watch' would be given other tasks for a few nights to enable the Jews to escape. Casper claimed 'Later Prince Oettingen phoned me that two Viennese Jewish ladies in Guernsey [Steiner and Spitz] refused to sail to England. They said all the Austrians in England were interned, also Jews.'; In 1997 Casper claimed 'Prince Oettingen further told me that the two Jewesses working in the Guernsey Hospital preferred to be interned in Germany as they were able to return home to Vienna which was their homeland.'

189 Longmate, If Britain Had Fallen, p.199

190 During their chance conversation Orange invited Bercu to attend his office to receive welfare/support benefit. Bercu remembers attending once but left immediately and did not return.

defence was that they had an overriding duty to remain in office in the interests of protecting the greatest number of the population. They considered that outright refusal to carry out all German orders would have simply resulted in their being removed from office and their authority usurped, having achieved little other than a point of principle. By co-operating in part, they accepted the inevitable consequence that this would result in individuals being substantially disadvantaged. Bailiff Coutanche stated: '*it would have been hopeless to take up the line with the Germans that they would have nothing to do with the anti-Jewish measures*'.

The authorities evolved a concept of duty to the community superseding an absolute obligation to an individual or small group of individuals. This concept was not restricted to the anti-Jewish measures, as is epitomised by the circumstances surrounding the discovery of prohibited wireless sets, belonging to non-Jewish island residents, by the Jersey police in June 1943. This case deserves detailed examination in this text as it encapsulates and illuminates many of the moral questions relevant to the registration and implementation of the measures against the Jews.

In August 1945, Jersey's Attorney-General prepared a report outlining the moral and legal dilemmas that had surrounded this discovery. The Jersey police officer involved had searched a house '*whilst investigating a robbery*'. The '*search proved of no value*' but during the '*interrogation of the persons concerned*' it came to the officer's '*knowledge'* that wireless sets were hidden at the property. The police officer returned to the house and discovered three hidden wireless sets which he '*sequestrated ...and placed ... in safe custody at the Parish Hall'*. He became concerned that as his investigations had been initiated '*by a neighbours quarrel..........there was a grave risk that knowledge of the police discovery of the wireless sets question would soon reach the ears of the Germans.*' The police officer sought the Attorney-General Aubin's advice as '*he was in doubt...where his duty lay; whether to report the facts, as was his legal obligation, and thus expose a civilian to prosecution or to conceal the facts and thus run the risk, in the event of the Germans discovering the facts, of the .... police administration being taken over by the Germans'*.

Aubin was not prepared to give a ruling on '*a matter in which considerations of conscience entered so strongly*' but he informed the police that if they presented a report to him he 'would have no alternative but to forward it to the Occupying Authority' as required under the 'Order for the protection of the Occupying Authority' registered in Jersey's Royal Court in February 1943. The Attorney-General considered that his overriding duty was to comply with this '*law of the Island'* which required that *'it shall be the duty of the local Law Officers to submit to the nearest German military tribunal all information brought to their knowledge and all records and other documents relating to .... infractions of orders made in the occupied territory .... for the purposes of the occupation'*.

The parish police considered the matter and *'their unanimous opinion was that the duty of the police was to the community rather than to the individual'* and thus a report was submitted to the Attorney-General which he in turn passed on to the Germans. Frederick Page, the owner of one of the wireless sets, after being tried by a German court was deported to Germany where he was subjected to hard labour and tragically died as a result of the mistreatment he received from the Nazis. [191]

In September 1942 when faced with the Order to deport mainland born British subjects against which there was no possibility of objection, Bailiff Coutanche again applied the principle of duty to the greater number. He remained in office *'in the interest of the people of Jersey'* and agreed to the local police providing a *'guide'* to locate those ordered for deportation.

In both the Frederick Page case and the 1942 deportations, the civilian authorities demonstrated the realisation that in the interest of the greater number moral ideas had to be compromised and they accepted the consequences of these pivotal decisions.

In the same context the civilian authorities subordinated their obligations to the few resident Jews. Their compliance in registering and implementing the anti-Jewish legislation was framed by the latitude they felt able to exercise within the constraints of their agreement in July 1940 to implement German legislation.

The pre-war residency applications of Jewish refugees provided the authorities with ample evidence of the mistreatment of Jews by the Nazis. Their compliance in registering the First Order was influenced by the inaccurate presumption that nearly all the Jews had left the islands. However, when faced with completed registration forms, the civilian authorities did not seek to provide mitigating evidence in support of those who in the strict terms of the Order may not have been *'deemed to*

---

[191] JAS D/ZLaw Officers Files; Attorney-General's memorandum of 4 Aug 1945 and associated correspondence; Frederick Page was sentenced to 21 months imprisonment for 'failing to surrender a wireless set'. At his trial Page maintained a steadfastly patriotic stance, boasting that he had fought the 'Hun' in the First World War. The German judge ordered his deportation. He was firstly imprisoned at Fort d'Hauteville, then Sabruchen before being transferred to Frankfurt-Preungesheim penal prison in January 1944 where he was subjected to forced hard labour. In July Page was transferred to Naumburg-on-Saale where rations consisted of a bowl of soup a day. He died on 5 Jan 1945 as a result of the mistreatment he had received in German prisons. (see Paul Saunders 'The Ultimate Sacrifice' P 16-20)

be Jews'. When faced with evidence of active discrimination against the registered Jews, the only protest against the remaining Orders was Bailiff Coutanche's appeal against the registration of the Yellow Star Order in Jersey.

There can be little doubt that the imprimatur of registering the laws in the Royal Courts, rather than their having been simply German decrees, encouraged those of Jewish origin to declare themselves. Furthermore there is no evidence indicating that Jews were discouraged from registering and without the involvement of the civilian authorities the Germans would have had much greater difficulty in identifying many of those '*deemed to be Jews*'.

When knowledge of the Holocaust began to unfold the fate of the islands Jews was largely overlooked by historians. Despite the fact that the anti-Jewish measures in the islands had led directly to deportation, extreme hardship and in some cases death, the fate of two dozen individuals resident on British soil may have seemed insignificant when compared to so many millions who perished in Europe. The members of the civilian authorities directly involved in the implementation of the anti-Jewish measures kept the subject 'closed' both during the war and after Liberation, contributing to much of the post-war speculation. Examination of the abundance of documentation now available, much of which has only recently surfaced, now enables the decisions of the civilian authorities to be more fully understood

Dr. Charles Cruickshank, commissioned by the governments of Jersey and Guernsey to write the 'Official History of the Occupation Years', concluded in relation to the anti-Jewish orders

> *'If the Islanders had refused to register the legislation it would have been promulgated by decree, but at least they would have made a stand. At what cost we cannot tell'*[192]

Sir Philip Bailhache, Bailiff of Jersey eloquently stated in his address at the 1998 Jersey Synagogue memorial service:

> *'the exercise of tyranny usually seeks to find a spurious legitimacy through laws and regulations. There is a duty therefore to scrutinise carefully legislation which restricts individual freedoms.'*

The civilian authorities' obligation to exercise diligence when passing discriminatory legislation was balanced against their obligations towards the majority of the populace. However, once the anti-Jewish Orders had

[192] Cruickshank, 'The German Occupation of the Channel Islands – The Official History of the Occupation Years' p.113

been registered, they had a clear moral obligation to use stealth and foresight in their implementation in order to minimise the consequences.[193]

The civilian authorities had endeavoured to act in the best interests of the majority of islanders. To prevent their offices being usurped they felt they had no option other than to register the German anti-Jewish Orders. However their implementation resulted in discrimination, deportation, despair, and premature death. Furthermore, the authorities decisions contrasted with those taken in relation both to the disclosure of British soldiers in hiding in 1940 and to the confiscation of Masonic property in 1941. However the principled and commendable objections of Sir Abraham Laine to the First Order and of Lord Coutanche to the Eighth Order, together with his life saving plea on behalf of Malherbe and Schwob, preclude any universal criticism of the civilian authorities.

The actions of Albert Bedane, Dorothea Weber, Bozena Kotyzova, Advocate Le Cornu, Advocate Poch and Edward Ogier, combined with the efforts to protect Jewish business interests and the absence of evidence of denunciation of undeclared Jews, entitle Islanders generally to worthy praise for protecting their fellow residents who were of Jewish origin.[194]

---

[193] The Sunday Telegraph, 14 May 2000 - David Feldman, the son of Louis Feldman and Rose Peretz whose businesses had been Aryanised stated 'The island authorities were seeking to fight only some battles and the Jews were a battle they did not fight. It is almost as if they were airbrushed out of Jersey citizenship'.

[194] The uncovering of Marianne Grunfeld in Guernsey in 1942, and the lack of surviving documentation concerning her discovery and subsequent deportation, leaves a small possibility that the German authorities uncovered other persons 'deemed to be Jews' in the islands and for which the evidence lies undiscovered.

POSTSCRIPT

In June 1946 Jersey's Defence Committee received a residency application from a Polish Jewish refugee and her three children. The Committee, likely following Home Office policy, advised the Bailiff 'The Island Defence Committee wish that they could recommend the application on compassionate grounds, but they feel that it should be refused in view of the acute shortage of living accommodation and the probability that, if it was granted, it would become the forerunner of several similar applications' (see JID States Greffier's Files).

In 1946 John Max Finkelstein applied for British Government support for the reinstatement of his Egyptian civil service pension. The Foreign Office informed the British Ambassador in Cairo that Mr Finkelstein was a 'technical enemy on two counts, as a Roumanian, and as having been in enemy territory'. The only period Finkelstein had been in 'enemy territory' was the 27 months he had spent incarcerated in concentration camps (see PRO HO 45/24756)

Maps, Documents and Photographs

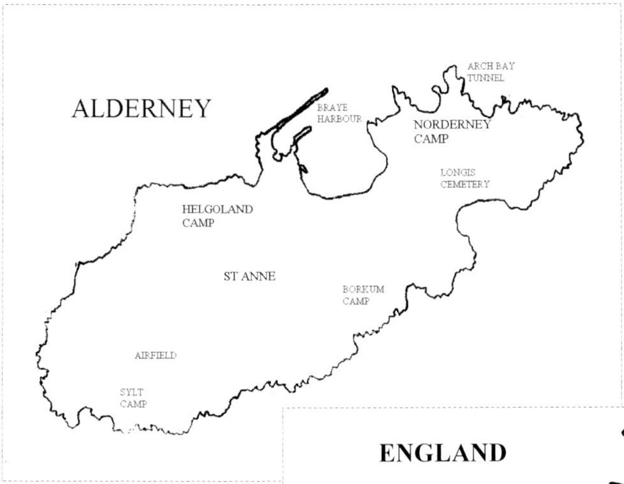

Alderney - the island is approximately 3 ½ miles by 1 mile

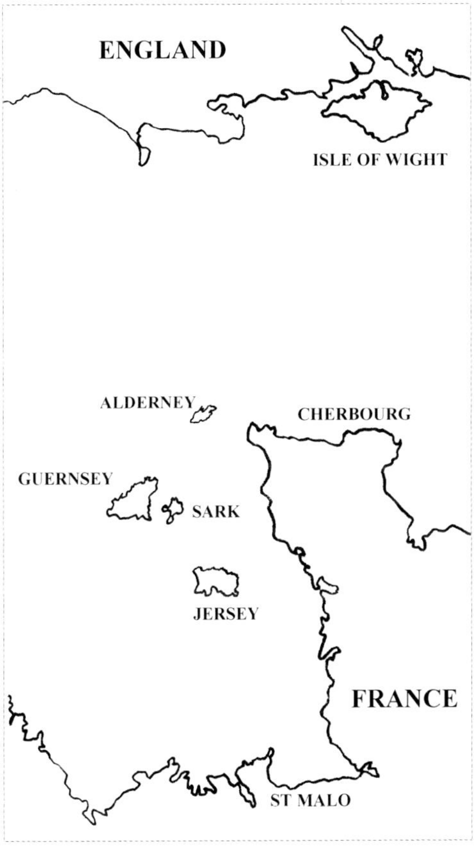

The Channel Islands, and the adjacent coasts of France and England

D.R.
1940
No. 156

NOTICE

concerning the registration of Jews in Jersey.

In pursuance of an Order* of the Chief of the German Military Administration in France (Registered by Act of the Royal Court, dated October 21st, 1940) and in virtue of the power delegated to me by the Bailiff, all Jews must present themselves for registration at the Aliens Office, No. 6, Hill Street, St. Helier, on Wednesday and Thursday, October 23rd and 24th, 1940, between the hours of 10 a.m. and 4 p.m.

For the purposes of this **Order, persons are deemed to be Jews who** belong or have belonged **to the Jewish religion or who have more than two Jewish grand parents.**

Grand parents who belong or have belonged to the Jewish religion are deemed to be Jews.

The particulars to be provided upon registration are :—

1. Surname.
2. Christian name.
3. Date of birth.
4. Place of birth.
5. Sex.
6. Family status.
7. Profession.
8. Religious faith.
9. Length of uninterrupted residence in the Island.

The declaration of the head of the family will suffice for the whole family.

CLIFFORD ORANGE,
Chief Aliens Officer.

October **21**st, 1940.

* No. 154.

50/10/40.

Appendix to the first 'Order relating to Measures against the Jews' registered in Jersey's Court October 1940

'Jewish Undertakings' sign in Krichefski's shop window

Therese Steiner

Auguste Spitz

Marianne Grunfeld

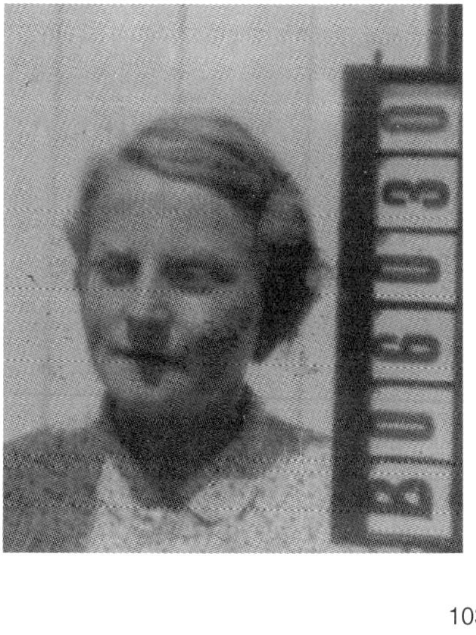

John Max Finkelstein

Elda Brouard

Elisabet Duquemin

Samuel Selig Simon

Hedwig Bercu – photograph and notice from the Jersey Evening Post after she went into hiding

NOTICE

The German authorities are looking for Miss Hedwig Bercu (see photograph), typist, of no nationality, 24 years of age, formerly residing at West Park, 1 Canon Tower. She has been missing from her residence since November 4th, 1943, and has evaded the German authorities. Any person who knows the whereabouts of Miss Bercu is requested to get in touch with the Feldkommandantur 515, who will treat any information with the strictest confidence. Anyone concealing Miss Bercu or aiding her in any other manner makes himself liable to punishment.

Die FELDKOMMANDANTUR.

Jersey, 17.11.1943.

Hyam Goldman

Esther Pauline Lloyd

Nathan Davidson

Ruby Still

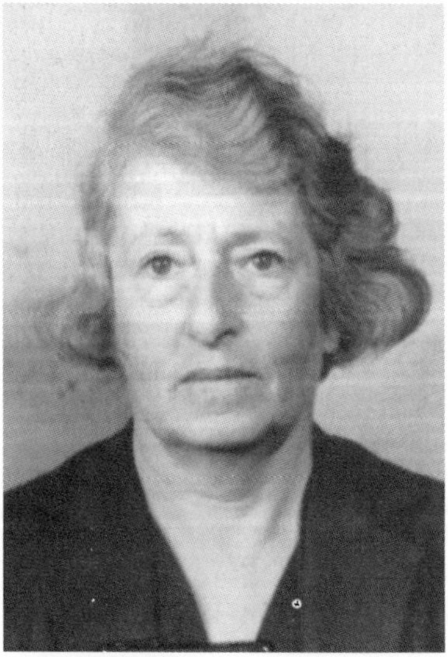

Marianne Blampied

Mary Erica Richardson

Yellow Star' found in Alderney and likely worn there by a Jewish forced worker of other than French nationality.

Jersey's Attorney-General instructs Nathan Davidson to close his grocery shop under the *Aryanization* of Jewish businesses program.

Davidson's reply confirming the closure of his shop

11th January, 1941.

Sir,

I refer to our recent interview regarding the Orders received from Field Command 515 regarding your business, and now have to inform you, as you have elected to close down rather than have an Aryan administrator appointed, that that authority requires your business to be wound up before January 25th, 1941.

I have to require you, therefore, to proceed to make your arrangements accordingly, and to inform me in writing when the winding up of your business is actually completed.

Yours faithfully,

[signature]

Attorney General.

Mr. N. Davidson,
35, Stopford Road,
St. Helier.

N. DAVIDSON
35. STOPFORD ROAD
St HELIER

January 23rd 1941

Sir

In accordance to your instructions I beg to inform you that I have finished the winding up of my Business at 35 Stopford Road. to day January 23rd 1941 the blind on the window pulled down and a notice 'CLOSED' displayed.

Yours truly

N Davidson
59. Oxford Road

ATTORNEY General's Chambers
JERSEY

Registration of Jews in Jersey.

1. Surname. DAVIDSON

2. Christian name. Nathan

3. Date of birth. 16th August 1881.

4. Place of birth. Roumania

5. Sex. Male

6. Family status. Married.

7. Profession. News Agent and Grocer.

8. Religious faith. Christian.

9. Length of uninterrupted residence in the Island. 5 years.

Note.
Mr. Davidson has stated that he has always belonged to the Christian community, & so far as he is aware, his father did also. Believes that one of his grandparents was a Jew, but knows nothing about the others. C.O.

N Davidson

Address: – 35, Stopford Road, St Helier.

Nathan Davidson's 'First Order' registration form. Signed by Nathan Davidson, but completed and annotated by Clifford Orange – Oct 1940. Similar forms were completed by all 11 registered Jews in Jersey

OKVR Dr Willhelm Casper. The senior German administrator of the anti-Jewish program in Jersey, Guernsey and Sark 1941-43

SS Hauptstrumfuhrer Maximilian List Commandant of Sylt Concentration Camp in Alderney

J.L.

THE CONTROLLING COMMITTEE OF THE STATES OF GUERNSEY.

HIRZEL HOUSE,

1/1/6
1/1/10

Guernsey.
30th October, 1941.

Feldkommandantur 515,
Nebenstelle,
Guernsey.

Dear Sir,

In response to your request to be notified of the "Key" Persons on the list submitted to you by the Bailiff on September 23th, I beg to submit the following names:-

Germany.	Steiner, Theresia	Nurse.
France.	Hollard, Pierre Paul	Interpreter.

The following are employed in Agriculture or Horticulture.

Germany.	Schlier, Else.
France.	Hemery, Alphonse Louis
	Simmoneux, Fridore M.
	Tanqueril, Maurice Jules
	Squeren, Francine.
Holland.	Honig, Cornelius.
	Winter, Jan
United States of America.	McGahy, Arthur William
Poland.	Grunsfeld, Marianne.

I should like to draw your attention to two points:-

1. A considerable number of names on the list submitted to you whom I have not included above are working for the German Authorities.

2. In the case of McGahy his wife Millicent and son Roy Arthur and in the case of Hollard his wife Jean Eva are on the list submitted to you.

Yours faithfully,

JOHN LEALE.

List of 'key aliens' provided by the Controlling Committee of the States of Guernsey to the Feldkommandantur in Oct 1941. This bears the names of Marianne Grunfeld, Therese Steiner and Millicent McGahy who were all deported on 21 April 1942. It was the likely source of the uncovering of Marianne Grunfeld

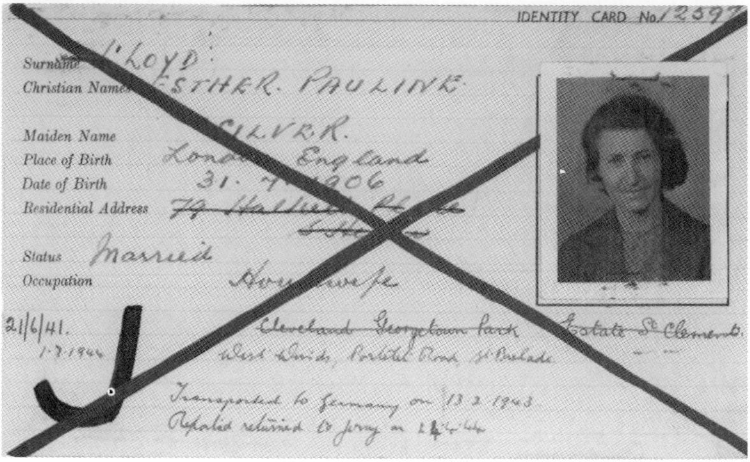
IDENTITY CARD No. 12597

Surname LLOYD

Christian Names ESTHER PAULINE

Maiden Name SILVER

Place of Birth London England

Date of Birth 31. 7. 1906

Residential Address

Status Married

Occupation Housewife

21/6/41. Cleveland Georgetown Park Estate St Clement.

1.7.1944 West Winds, Portelet Road, St Brelade

Transported to Germany on 13.2.1943

Reported returned to Jersey on

March 1941 the Germans order 'The filing cards of all Jewish persons are to be specially marked and this marking is to consist of a large red J in a conspicuous position and the cards are also to have a red cross strip'

Esther Pauline Lloyd's registration card (top)

Margarete Hurban's registration card (bottom)

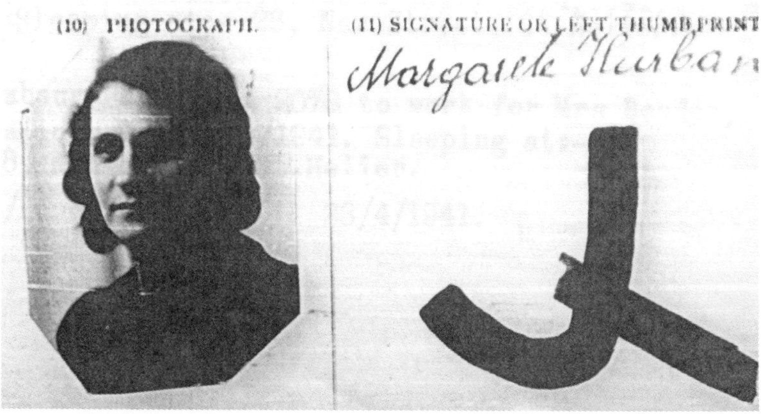
(10) PHOTOGRAPH.

(11) SIGNATURE OR LEFT THUMBPRINT

Margarete Hurban

Sir Abraham Laine (centre)

Bailiff Alexander Coutanche and Attorney-General Charles Aubin meet the German command at Jersey airport

W30/96.

15.vi.42. Visited Dr Casper, with A.G. We advised that this Order should not be registered or put into execution.

Dr Casper agreed I should take no further action at present. A.M.C.

The Bailiff of Jersey's note detailing his successful intervention in relation to the registration of the 'Jewish Star' Order

30th June 1942.

Dear Madam,

I am directed by the Bailiff to forward to you herewith for your information copy of an Order made by the German Authorities entitled "Eighth Order regarding Measures against Jews" dated May 29th, 1942, and registered on the Records of this Island on to-day's date.

Yours faithfully,

Greffier.

Copy sent to Mrs. E. Duquemin, Cobo Post Office, Castel and Mrs. Elda Brouard, "Electra", Belmont Road.

Letter from the Greffier of the States of Guernsey dated 30 June 1942 notifying Elda Brouard and Elisabet Duquemin of the registration of the 'Jewish Star' Order and enclosing a translated copy of the Order

Abdruck.

Feldkommandantur 515
- Mil.Verw.Gr. -
Az.: Pol.02 - 4.
Li.

Jersey, den 17.6.1942.

An den

Höheren SS- und Polizeiführer

Paris.

Betr.: Kennzeichnung der Juden.
Bezug: Erlass vom 1.6.1942 - S Pol.IV J - 221 b.

Ich habe die Staaten von Jersey und Guernsey veranlasst, die 8. Verordnung über Massnahmen gegen Juden vom 28.Mai 1942 zu registrieren, d.h. zu staatseigenen Gesetzen der Inselstaaten zu machen.

Es sind hier nur eine geringe Anzahl Juden vorhanden u.zw.

a) auf Jersey: 7 Juden britischer Staatsangehörigkeit,
1 Jude ägyptischer "
1 " deutscher "
2 " rumänischer " ;

b) auf Guernsey: 2 Juden britischer Staatsangehörigkeit.

Der angezogene Erlass vom 1.6.42 besagt nun, dass nur solche der Kennzeichnung unterliegen, deren Heimatländer ähnliche Massnahmen durchgeführt haben. Hierbei sind nicht die Juden britischer Staatsangehörigkeit aufgeführt. Ich bitte daher um Entscheidung, ob auch diese Juden den Judenstern zu tragen haben.

Ggf. bitte ich um Beschaffung der entsprechenden Anzahl von Judensternen mit dem Aufdruck "Jew".

Für den Feldkommandanten

gez. Dr. Casper
O.K.V.R.

JUN 20 1942

Abdruck an

Nebenstelle Guernsey
der F.K.515

Guernsey

zur Kenntnis.

Für den Feldkommandanten

Dr. Casper
O.K.V.R.

OKVR Dr Casper informs the Higher SS and Police Leaders in Paris of the number and nationalities of the registered Jews in the Islands. Casper seeks confirmation that the order covers British Jews and concludes 'I kindly ask you to send the required number of Jewish stars with the word 'Jew'' (emblazoned in English)

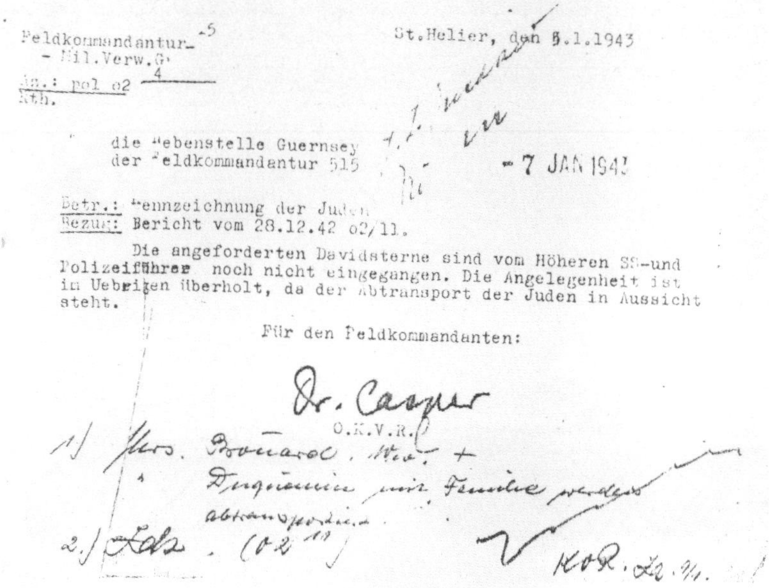

Feldkommandantur-5
- Mil.Verw.Gr.
Az.: pol o2 4
Ath.

St.Helier, den 5.1.1943

die Nebenstelle Guernsey
der Feldkommandantur 515

- 7 JAN 1943

Betr.: Kennzeichnung der Juden
Bezug: Bericht vom 28.12.42 o2/11.

Die angeforderten Davidsterne sind vom Höheren SS-und Polizeiführer noch nicht eingegangen. Die Angelegenheit ist im Uebrigen überholt, da der Abtransport der Juden in Aussicht steht.

Für den Feldkommandanten:

Dr. Casper
O.K.V.R.

1.) Mrs. Brouard, Mrs. + Duquemin mit Familie werden abtransportiert.
2.) Zdа. (o2 11)

Dr Casper's letter to the Guernsey Nebenstelle of 5 Jan 1943
'The Jewish stars that have been requested from the Higher SS and Police leader have not yet arrived. The matter in any case is superseded as the deportation of the Jews is in sight'. *In handwriting* 'Mrs Brouard and Mrs Duquemin and family are to be deported'

Transportliste für Lager Compiègne

Lfd. Nr.	Name	Vorname	Geb.	Grund der Evakuierung
63	Bachmann	Elste Maude	21.4.88	Offiziersfrau
64	Chilcott	Victoria Trixie	13.4.94	"
65	Dumont	Marjorie Lorna	28.1.97	"
66	Giraud	Margaret Mary	24.3.94	"
67	Giraud	Margaret Anne	12.9.23	" Tochter
68	Nichols	Ellen Marion	21.9.95	"
9	Pomeroy	Lizzie Louisa	14.12.83	"
7o	Way	Bertha Annie	6.2.oo	"
71	Bartlett	Lily Freda	6.6.93	"
72	Bartlett	Robin Luff Bart.	1o.7.37	" Kind 5½ Jhr.
73	Gill	Marjorie Frances	1o.11.24	vorbestraft
74	Oliver	Olive May	15.2.9o	Mann pol.unzuvl.
75	Foss	Mary Margaret	25.6.82	Mann Geistl.
76	Foss	Dulcie Margaret	4.5.19	Vater Geistl.
77	Foss	Henry	21.11.78	Geistlicher über 64 Jh.
78	Duquemin	Elizabeth	21.7.oo	Jüdin
79	Duquemin	Janet	9.6.41	Kind 19 Mt.alt)
1o6	Brouard	Elda	27.4.84	Jüdin
24	Duquemin	Henry Edward	24.6.98	Frau Juedin

The Feldkommandantur's lists of those to be deported from Guernsey in Feb 1943 stating in each case the specific reason for selection. In Elisabet Duquemin and Elda Brouard's case the stated reason is 'Jew' and in Henry Duquemin's case 'Wife is a Jew'. Janet Duquemin aged 19 months is also listed.

Arthur Samuel and Martha Helga Kleinstein

'Star of David' moulded into the concrete of a German fortification in Alderney by a Jewish forced worker

The marked Jewish graves at Longis cemetery in Alderney in 1945. The memorial board erected by the British Liberating forces read 'Here lie the bodies of eight French Nationals of the Jewish faith who died during the German occupation'. Their remains were subsequently exhumed and reburied in France

M. Theodore Haenel, a French Jewish survivor of Norderney camp in Alderney photographed in May 1998 at the Hammond memorial after leading the Jewish memorial prayers dedicated to his fellow forced workers at the annual memorial service.

Mr Jon Kay-Mouat OBE, President of the States of Alderney addresses the 1998 Memorial Service at the Jersey Synagogue.
Other speakers seated from left: Rev. Malcolm Weisman OBE, Visiting Minister V. Rev. John Seaford, Dean of Jersey: Lord Jakobovits, Emeritus Chief Rabbi: Frederick Cohen, President of the Jersey Jewish Congregation: Sir Philip Bailhache, Bailiff of Jersey: Sir Graham Dorey, Bailiff of Guernsey

Westmount Slave Worker Memorial, St Helier, Jersey. The plaque to Jewish slave workers (bottom left) reads 'To the memory of the Jews who suffered during the Occupation'

Part 2

Jewish forced labourers transported to the Channel Islands during the German Occupation

Jewish forced labourers transported to the Channel Islands during the German Occupation

Introduction

Throughout occupied Europe the Germans rounded up Jews and pressed them into forced labour.[195] This text is intended to chronicle the experiences of the Jewish forced workers transported to the Channel Islands during the Occupation and to place this within the context of the experiences of forced workers of all nationalities and religions.[196] Sources used include survivor testimony and interviews, together with documents at the Centre de Documentation Juive Contemporaine, Moscow State Archives, Yad Vashem, the Jersey and Guernsey Archive Services and the Public Records Office.

Much of the source documentation of the Organisation Todt, Wehrmacht and SS was destroyed in the final months of the war.[197] However important records have recently resurfaced, including General Basilov's report on the atrocities in Alderney submitted to the [Soviet] Emergency State Commission for the Investigation and Establishment of Fascist Crimes in April 1947. This report, uncovered by Madeleine Bunting, was declassified by the Moscow State archives in 1993 and includes the only known surviving copy of Major (then Captain) Theodore Pantcheff's 'Official British government report about the atrocities on Alderney' completed after interrogating 1,500 German Prisoners of War in Guernsey, 1,200 in Jersey and 500 in Alderney. This report is the most important document in this area of research and significantly, it confirms the accuracy of many of the statements of horrific torture later made by survivors.

[195] Estimates of the total number of OT workers of all nationalities and religions transported to the Channel Islands vary. A German memorandum dated June 1942 lists 11,800 in the Islands at that time. Other German records list 16,000 in total comprising 6,700 in Guernsey, 5,300 in Jersey and 4,000 in Alderney in May 1943. In November 1943 another list records 2,890 in Guernsey, 3,746 in Jersey and 2,233 in Alderney. In July 1944 a list records 489 in Guernsey, 83 in Jersey and 245 in Alderney: Cruickshank, The German Occupation of the Channel Islands, pp.203-5.

[196] Other accounts of the fate of forced workers can be found in Bunting, The Model Occupation; Pantcheff, Alderney Fortress Island; Bonnard, Alderney at War.

[197] Organisation Todt (OT) was established under the direction of Dr Fritz Todt in the 1930s to provide labour for public construction projects in Germany. During the war it became the administration for providing forced, slave, conscripted and voluntary labour for many projects of the Reich including the construction projects in the Channel Islands. Organisation Todt did not formally take over control of the fortification and engineering protects in the Islands until between July-November 1941; Joe Miere, the former curator of the German Underground Hospital, remembered workers transporting documents for burning just before the end of the Occupation.

Despite the rediscovery of this report no definitive figure is available of the total number of workers who lost their lives either through ill-treatment in the Islands or subsequent to their transportation from the Islands by the Germans. Surviving burial lists record the graves of only around 750 workers who died in Jersey, Guernsey and Alderney.

The post-war war crimes investigations linked to the perpetrators of the crimes carried out during this period are not fully covered here.[198]

Forced workers arrive in the Channel Islands

In the spring of 1941 the Germans began an immense construction program of military defence structures in the Channel Islands. The workers transported to the Islands to construct these fortifications comprised a number of specific categories including conscripted, voluntary, forced and slave workers. Known Jews were in the forced or slave worker categories.

On 19 March 1941 Leslie Sinel in Jersey, noted in his diary the arrival *of 'Labour Corps and conscripted labour*'. Two weeks later Sinel wrote: '*there are working in the Island 100 labourers of various nationalities subject to Germany*'.[199]

The Reverend Douglas Ord in Guernsey recorded in August 1941: '*More rumours: the airport is to be doubled in extent. A thousand Frenchmen, Poles, Czechs and other nationalities enslaved by the Germans are to be brought over to do the job*'. In October Reverend Ord noted: '*Numbers of young Frenchmen are being brought over to labour on the fortifications. They look more than half starved already.*'[200] In the following month Leslie Sinel wrote: '*Germans are absolutely pouring in, including civilians*' and in December he noted: '*Thousands of foreign workers are being poured into the Island; these are of all nationalities ...; the majority of these workers are very poor specimens – badly clad and shod, and all of them terribly hungry ... if they got the chance they are always ready to beg for a bit of bread; the Germans keep strict supervision over them ...*'.[201]

[198] The war crimes investigations are covered in Bunting, The Model Occupation, and Pantcheff, Alderney Fortress Island.
[199] Leslie Sinel diary entry, 31 March 1941
[200] Reverend Ord diary entry, 30 Oct 1941
[201] Leslie Sinel diary entries, 7 Nov 1941 and 31 Dec 1941

The first Jewish Forced Workers transported to the Channel Islands

Many Jewish forced workers were included in these early groups of forced labourers transported to the Channel Islands. Many of the forced workers who began the tunnelling works in mid-1942 on what become known as the German Underground Hospital in Jersey were Jews from Poland, Czechoslovakia and Alsace-Lorraine. [202]

Pomar Pascal a founder member of the 'Federation Nationale Deportes Internes Resistants Patriotes' wrote to the administrators of the German Underground Hospital in Jersey commenting on the museum displays:

> *'In the history of slavery practised by the Nazis, there are omissions because you mention only Russians*[203]*...*
>
> *Now, I am in a good position to assure you that the first deportees to work on this site were Spanish Republicans, also a group of Polish, Czecho-Slovak and Alsatian Jews [from Alsace-Lorraine] arrested in the Toulouse area.*
>
> *These deportees imprisoned in Fort Regent, which the Germans called 'Lager Ehrembrestein' were transferred by lorry and worked from 4.00am to 7.00pm, so it was they who opened the first galleries.*
>
> *When the Russians arrived at the end of 1942, the work had progressed well. It is true that many Russians were employed in these tunnels and in inhumane conditions, which were the same for us all, but the first victims were Spanish and Jews (French, Polish etc.)*
>
> *So, in respect to all these victims and to history, it is indispensable that Spanish and Jews should be mentioned ...'*[204]

As there are no known Jewish survivors of this group of forced workers we must turn to an account by non-Jewish Ukrainian to describe the conditions encountered at the time. Vasilly Marempolsky, now a Professor of Literature in Zaporozhye, eastern Ukraine was transported to Jersey as a forced worker in August 1942 at the age of 16:

> *'After we landed on Jersey, I was taken to Lager Immelman on the west coast near St Ouens. The camp consisted of only six*

[202] The area now known as the German Underground Hospital, St Lawrence, Jersey comprises a substantial labyrinth of tunnels begun in 1942 probably partly as an ordnance depot. Later part was designated as a hospital for the German forces but it was never completed.

[203] The forced workers generally referred to as 'Russians' usually comprised many nationalities including Ukrainians and Poles.

[204] Pomar Pascal sent two versions, the first in French on 7 Sept. 1970 and a later English translation dated 10 Sept. 1970.

huts and was surrounded by two rows of barbed wire. In the huts there were three wooden platforms, one on top of the other, which served as beds; there was a bit of straw on them, but no blankets. There were about five to six hundred people in the camp, and we were organised into working units of fifty men. We nicknamed the guard who was in charge of our unit 'Cherni' - 'the Black' - because he had black hair.

We got up at five o'clock and had dirty black water called coffee. After breakfast, we heard the whistle and we had to stand to attention for the Germans; those who were slow were beaten. We were building a railway and we had to level the ground. Sometimes we had to crush rocks. Between one and two o'clock we had a lunch break and we were given turnip 'soup'; it was water with a tiny lump of turnip in it. We usually worked for twelve or fourteen hours a day. The Germans watched us from behind, and as soon as anyone paused to straighten their back, they would beat him. We had to stay bent over and pretend to work all the time. Then the Germans got wise to that and watched to see if we were working hard enough. If they decided we weren't, the Germans would beat us.

At the end of the day, we all received tiny cards with 'supper' printed on them. This entitled us to half a litre of soup and 200 grams of 'bread' which had bits of wood in it. Every second Sunday we had a day off and then we didn't get any food because we weren't working.

Sometimes as we marched back to camp, we would steal a turnip or a beetroot. Sometimes an Islander would put out some bread or proper soup for us. I never knew the islanders' names but we knew they had a lot of sympathy for us. Within a few months of arriving, my jacket had disintegrated. As we marched past a farm I saw some people waiting by a gate. One of them was an island girl and she had a big jacket and she threw it over my shoulders. It was very useful.

Lice were a great problem because there was no disinfectant. People began to catch illnesses like typhus and dysentery and many people died of exhaustion.[205] *By the end of October I couldn't walk, I was so weak from exhaustion and dysentery, but*

[205] A typhus epidemic is recorded amongst foreign workers in the Islands in late 1941 (Alan and Mary Wood, Islands in Danger, London 1965, P159). The Reverend D. Ord refers to other epidemics in Sept 1942 and Feb 1943 amongst 'foreign workers' in Guernsey resulting the deaths of thirty.

my friends helped me. One day I had stayed behind when the others went to work and I went to the camp medicine post. A Spanish doctor and nurse at this post took me to a hospital the Spanish had set up for the foreign workers. A Spaniard took pity on me and nursed me back to life; his name was Gasulla Sole. A Jersey woman also came to the hospital to give me bread.

When I was better I had to go back to Lager Immelman. The men had begun work on the underground hospital. We thought it might be some kind of mine but it had no coal. We had to march from the camp to the underground hospital every day. About a quarter of our brigade died, and they were replenished by men from another camp on Jersey.

It was barely light when we began the march to the underground hospital. We were very young boys, we were thin, exhausted, dressed in torn clothes and blue with cold. The worksite was a huge labyrinth of tunnels. I was terrified. The roof was supported by wooden props in some places and we could hear running water and smell damp. It felt like a grave. The walls were rough-hewn and there was mud underfoot. Everywhere there were people working like ants. It was hard to believe all these tunnels had been dug out by the weakening hands and legs of these slaves. People were so frail, they could barely lift a spade. The future for everyone was the same - death.'[206]

In an autobiographical account of his experiences, published only in Ukrainian, Vasilly Marempolsky recounted the kindness shown to him by a Jersey farming family and indicated how this had sustained him during periods of despair:

'The farmer moved a chair to a table under a big tree and offered me a seat. The farmers wife brought a plate of mashed potato and some pieces of white bread. I looked incredulously at the farmer, his wife and their daughter, and they were nodded their heads inviting me to eat. Never in my life had potato with butter tasted so wonderful! Then I remembered about "Black" who would be looking for me any minute and quickly used the fork. I quickly drank a quarter of milk and put the bread in the pocket.

[206] Author's correspondence with Vasilly Marempolsky 1998-9; Madeleine Bunting interview with Vasilly Marempolsky (The Model Occupation, p. 155-158)

> *"Spasibo!(*"thank you" in Ukrainian) Merci! Danke shon!" I bowed to the hospitable owners who were looking at me with pity.*
>
> *The landlord was saying something to me, waving his hand. Even though I did not understand the language I guessed by his intonation and honesty that I was being invited to visit them again. I nodded my head, agreeing, and run to the embankment of the road.*
>
> *During the two and a half months that I suffered in "Immelman" nobody spared any kind words. Everyday I only saw the raging eyes of "Black", heard his endless swearing, and endured his kicks and blows. Exhausting 22 hours work (sic), continuous hunger and nonstop thoughts about food! And yet it seemed that even there on that half-wild island there lived people who sympathised with a poor slave. And each new day the work was no easier: the same labouring with the crowbar, collecting rocks into the trolley, pain in the waist, crazy shouting by "Black", who was always beating somebody over the shoulders ... but I was far away from it. Inwardly I was thinking of a farmer and his wife and daughter'.*

Marempolsky's account of the kindness shown to him by Islanders was not unique. John Dalmau wrote '*I shall never forget the kindness shown to me and the other slave workers by the people of Jersey*'. Many Jersey men and women hid escaped forced workers and some paid for their compassion with their lives. One, Louisa Gould died at Ravensbrück having been denounced for sheltering a forced worker. [207]

Jewish forced workers were also among the workers transported to Guernsey in late 1941 and 1942. Further groups of Jewish slave workers were recorded in Guernsey in September 1943.[208]

Elie Binder a Jew who had been rounded up in Luxembourg was transported to the Islands as a forced worker and worked on German fortifications in both Jersey and Guernsey.[209] It is also probable that Jews were amongst the forced workers transported to Sark as a Yellow Star marked 'Juif' was found in the Island after the war.[210]

---

[207] A German order of Nov. 1942 stated 'the public are warned not to come into close contact with these foreign workers'; Louisa Gould's brother, also deported for aiding a slave worker, was the sole British survivor of Belsen

[208] Julia Tremayne 'War on Sark' Webb and Bower, Exeter, 1981 notes Jewish forced workers in Guernsey in 1943 (p.151 entry for 1 Sept 1943)

[209] Author's interviews with Max Geshaft and John Miller

[210] A number of fortifications were constructed in Sark, including works in the area of the harbour and tunnels near Stocks Hotel. A group of forced workers were transported to the

The Reverend Douglas Ord's diary records to *'foreign slaves'* in Guernsey on a number of occasions and he witnessed transportations from '*Continental*' cities in April 1942. In May 1942 Ord wrote: '*Many are now in a most repulsive condition. All are treated like cattle by their German taskmasters ... [they are] at work on a light railway ... It is repulsive to note the squalor of these poor wretches*'.

The Medical Officer of Health in Guernsey noted in his 1941 report that '*foreign slaves*' were held in overcrowded and insanitary conditions in St Peter Port. In September 1942 Reverend Ord recorded the departure of '*Hundreds of foreign slaves*' in terrible physical condition. In the following week he noted the arrival of replacement workers. Reverend Ord records the arrival of further groups of forced workers in February 1943.[211]

In Jersey, Superior Council member Edward Le Quesne witnessed forced workers being transported back to the European mainland to an unknown fate.

> *'14 September 1942 – A terrible sight was witnessed today. Several Russian prisoners being returned to France passed down the pier. These men definitely seriously ill were without boots or stockings and were compelled to drag themselves along with seven German bullies hurrying them on as if they were cattle'*

Perhaps however, Edward Le Quesne's most poignant diary reference relates to an event he witnessed on 19 February 1943

> *'not Russia or Poland but Jersey. A Russian in the pillory at Morville, St Ouens with two branches of trees tied tightly round his neck and attached to two trees., the man just able to touch the ground with his toes.... Some of us had imagined that the tales we had heard of similar atrocities in Russia were simply for propaganda purposes. Now we have witnessed them in Jersey we are less sceptical'.*

Gordon Prigent a non-Jewish forced worker at Norderney estimated that workers remained in the Islands for only nine months after which they were in such poor condition that they were largely incapable of work and were transported back to the European mainland. Gasulla Sole, a Spanish worker testified that sick prisoners '*were taken off Jersey in Belgian boats which had been used for transporting cement*'. Statements

island at this time and the proprietor of the Sark Occupation museum stated that they were housed near the prison. The Yellow Star is now on display at the Sark Occupation Museum..

[211] Rev Ord diary 11 Sept 1942: Rev. Ord noted on 16 Dec. 1942 that many 'foreign slaves' were poorly 'housed' in George Street, St Peter Port.

by SS Obersturmführer Kurt Klebeck and SS Hauptsturmführer Maximilian List confirm that large numbers of exhausted forced workers were transported to extermination camps in Occupied Europe.[212]

Jewish Forced Workers in Alderney

Transportations of labourers to Alderney, including Jewish forced workers, began in early 1942. Many of the Jews in the early transportations had been arrested in the Paris area. Together with German political prisons they laboured at the docks, in building machine shops and in making the Lower Road. These workers were housed in vacated Islanders homes in a wired off section of Newtown.

Four main camps were constructed for OT workers in Alderney: Norderney, Helogoland, Borkum and Sylt, in addition to a smaller camp, Citadella.[213] Sylt, came under the control of the Totenkopfverbank (Death's Head) section of the SS in March 1943. The camp was designated SS Baubrigade 1 and formed a sub-camp of Neuengamme

---

212 G. Sole's recorded testimony at the Imperial War Museum; The courts-marshal documents of SS Obersturmführer Kurt Klebeck at SS Hauptsturmführer Maximilian List held at the Berlin Document Centre confirm that many 'worked out' and sick workers were sent back to the European mainland for 'extermination'.

However some members of a group of sick workers were spared. In late 1942 news of the 'inhumane treatment' of the prisoners in Alderney reached Guernsey and orders were sent to Oberst Zuske the Alderney Commandant to instigate an inquiry. St. Feldw. Kurt Busse stated that together with, Wilhelm Reinhold and a Medical Officer he inspected Lager Helgoland. Ob. Feldw. Roeder and two other officers inspected Lager Norderney.

An MI 19 interrogation report of a number of Russians brought back from Cherbourg in 1944 states that as a result of this inquiry 800 sick prisoners in Alderney were transported to France. The Russians stated to MI 19 investigators that on arrival in France 450 of the sick prisoners were hospitalised and others put to 'lighter' work.

However Albert Pothugine, a survivor of the transportation ships Xaver Dorsch and Franka, stated that the transportation became stranded on the Alderney rocks and for fourteen days the prisoners were kept below deck without food or water in appalling conditions without adequate sanitation, around 15 died.

The inspection commission had little long term effect, brutality and undernourishment escalated. SS Baubrigade 1 arrived at Sylt in March 1943 and transportations to extermination camps commenced in July. (PRO WO 208/3629 and WO 199/2090B-50157; Moscow State Archives V1 PW 15(H) LDC/477; Capt. T. Pantcheff 'Official British government report about the atrocities on Alderney', Moscow State Archives; Trial Documents of Maximilian List and Kurt Klebeck; Statement of POW Walter Schuller WO 208/3629

213 PRO WO 208/3629: St. Feldw. Kurt Busse in a statement to war investigators stated that the first Russians arrived in Alderney in June/July 1942, some being sent to Norderney, others to Helgoland. Prior to that Dutch and French were held at Helgoland. Dutch workers were also held at Borkum; T. Pantcheff in his 1946 report held at the Moscow State Archives records that in 1943 Borkum was used primarily for German conscripted OT workers. Pantcheff also noted that in July 1942 a group of about 1,000 Russian, Pole and Ukrainian forced workers were transported to Alderney followed by a further two groups totalling 1,800 in August 1942; PRO WO 208/3629: Grenadier Walter Schuller stated that Norderney and Helgoland were completed by mid 1942. He stated that a number of Spanish Republicans were held there. At the end of 1942 German workers were transferred to Borkum.

concentration camp in north Germany. 1,000 prisoners were initially transferred to Sylt from Sachsenhausen concentration camp including 500 Russians, 130 Poles, 60 Dutch, 20-30 Czechs, 20 French, and 180 German '*work-shy*', criminals and political prisoners. During the transportation to Alderney the prisoners were forced to work clearing bomb damage in Düsseldorf and Hamburg.[214]

Other prisoners were transferred to Sylt from other camps in Alderney as a punishment. OT Bauleiter Leo Ackermann testified to war crimes investigators that SS Haupstrumführer Maximilian List and OT Oberbauleiter Cardinal who was based in Cherbourg, had agreed to the transfer to Sylt of prisoners due for punishment from the other camps in Alderney. OT Haupttruppfuhrer Johann Hoffmann, Commandant of Helgoland camp stated that in early 1943 70-75 '*Russian*' prisoners were transferred to Sylt. When released in December they were in a '*terribly emaciated*' state and 10 to 15 died. Between May and August 1943 sixty forced workers were transferred from Norderney to Sylt.[215]

At Sylt horrific atrocities are recorded; a British Intelligence report stated:

> *'Any Russian defaulter was liable to transfer to this camp. One such was crucified on the camp gate, naked and in midwinter. The German guards threw buckets of cold water over him all night until he was dead. Another was caught by bloodhounds when attempting to stow away to the mainland. He was hanged and crucified on the same gate. His body was left hanging on the gate for 5 days as a warning'.*

Another report recorded:

> *'In mid-May 1943 four 'Russians' cut up a lamb to stave off hunger and for this they were bound by their hands to the main gates and the camp guard beat them ... many camp prisoners were starving and underwent terrible, wicked treatment. Witness statements show that many prisoners would walk around the rubbish pits of the slaughter house and pick up the offal. Six dogs were kept in the camp to frighten prisoners ... At work the prisoners were beaten every day, the majority by the*

---

[214] Capt. T. Pantcheff 'Official British government report about the atrocities on Alderney', Moscow State Archives; PRO WO 199/3303 notes that 948 prisoners were sent to Alderney on 3 March 1943.

[215] PRO HO 144/45; Pantcheff, Alderney Fortress Island, Chichester, p.32; PRO WO 208/3629 Interrogation of Johann Burbach - confirms that some of the prisoners transferred to Sylt from other camps in Alderney had been transferred for 'crimes such as the theft of food'. They were accommodated in a hut separate from the other prisoners .

> *Meister. There were frequent deaths of prisoners at work, in the harbour and returning from work.'* [216]

Considerable information is available on the Jews transported from France imprisoned at Norderney camp from mid-1943. However with fewer survivors, less information is available on the Jewish forced workers in other Alderney camps. Only a few survivor accounts are available complemented by various references to Jewish workers in MI 19 interrogation reports.[217]

Although the exact number of Jews held at the Sylt camp is unknown the Basilov/Pantcheff report and Pantcheff's own published account provide a few references relating to the period after March 1943 when the camp was under the control of the SS. Major Pantcheff details the feud over authority between the senior Organisation Todt official in Alderney, OT Bauleiter Leo Ackermann[218] and SS Haupstrumführer Maximilian List, senior officer at the Sylt camp. Ackermann, although well known for his brutal treatment of OT prisoners, complained to island Commandant Zuske about the way the SS '*beat their [Sylt] prisoners*' whilst working on the Organisation Todt work sites '*so that their capacity for work might be adversely affected*'. Pantcheff wrote:

> *'[Ackermann] then protested in writing to Fortress Engineer Staff, who referred the protest back to the SS. One of the beaten prisoners had been a Jew and so Ackermann now found himself the object of a counter complaint by the SS that he was soft on Jews. He had the good fortune to have this firmly resisted by the senior OT engineer in the Cherbourg Oberbauleitung and the matter was not proceeded with.'*[219]

---

[216] PRO WO 106/5248B (interview 2253); Moscow State Archives, V1 PW 15(H) LDC/477.

[217] PRO WO 106/5248B contains a report on the interrogation of two Guernseymen who had worked in Alderney. They stated that Helgoland was the main camp for Jewish workers. MI 19 interrogation report on interviews with three Russian OT workers also stated that Jews were held at Helgoland before being transferred to Norderney in Feb. 1944. However, whilst there may well have been individual Jewish prisoners in the camp it is unlikely that it was specifically a Jewish camp.

T. Misiewicz stated that he and other prisoners had been moved from Norderney to Helgoland to make room for the French Jews who arrived at Norderney in mid 1943. OT Haupttruppführer Johann Hoffmann stated that 'between September/October 1943 and January 1944, all the Russians except about 20 were evacuated from Helgoland Camp ... In March 1944, Helgoland camp was disbanded and transferred to Norderney'.

[218] Pantcheff noted 'During the second half of 1942 and the beginning of 1943 the Bauleiter was Johann Buthmann ... After two brief periods between March and September 1943 the post was held by Leo Ackermann until the final withdrawal of the OT in summer 1944': Alderney Fortress Island, p.7.

[219] Capt. T. Pantcheff 'Official British government report about the atrocities on Alderney', Moscow State Archives; Pantcheff, Alderney Fortress Island, p.31.

Reuven Freidman, a Norderney Jewish forced worker, also remembered the OT officers and the army having constantly disagreed over questions of authority over prisoners.

A. Wegmann, a German prisoner of war in Allied hands in 1945, further confirmed that Jews were amongst the prisoners at Sylt. Further, Wilhelm Wernegau, a German prisoner at Sylt stated that he knew of one Jewish political prisoner transferred in the initial contingent from Sachsenhausen concentration camp. He stated that this prisoners religion was not known to the SS.

A number of those broadly classified as 'Russians' were in fact Jews. Norbert Beernaert, a Belgium non-Jew, testified '*The Russians were all Ukrainians, one of whom was Jewish. He was revealed by the Ukrainians to the Germans and he was dead within a couple of days. I do not know how he died.*'[220]

John Dalmau a Spanish forced worker in Alderney in 1943 encountered many Jewish forced workers including a Romanian Jew. Jews were also amongst the North African prisoners held in Alderney.[221] A yellow star found in Alderney after the war emblazoned with the word '*Jude*' rather than the French '*Juif*' would suggest that it likely belonged to a Jewish forced worker of other than French nationality.

In July, August, October and December 1943 the main transportations of Jewish forced workers from France to Alderney took place. Serge Klarsfeld, the foremost authority on the fate of French Jewry during the Holocaust, has identified 700 French Jews sent to Alderney. It would seem that the total number transferred was around 1,000.[222]

Two Guernseymen who escaped to England in April 1944 and who had previously worked as fishermen in Alderney, stated in an MI 19 interrogation report '*There are about 1,000 Jews working for the Germans. These are mainly French and wear the yellow star with the word JUIF across it.*'[223]

The Jews transported from France at this time were predominantly middle-class well educated professionals, including many doctors, lawyers, musicians and teachers. In addition to French Jews the transportations included Jews originating from other countries occupied

---

[220] PRO WO 199/3303 (a)D15/86 MI19 intelligence report, 20 April 1945; Steckoll, The Alderney Death Camp, pp.81, 177.

[221] Dalmau, 'Slave Worker'; Advocate Anita Regal met a Jewish North African survivor of Alderney when attending the Alderney Memorial service in 1970; Steckoll records Moroccan prisoners at Citadella camp (p.27)

[222] Solomon Steckoll concluded 900 French Jews, Theodore Haenel 800-900.

[223] PRO WO 199/2090A (interview 50157)

by Germany including Poles, Czechs and Russians.[224] The majority of the Jews transported from France to Alderney at this time were married to non-Jews and thus classified as '*Conjoint D'Aryenne'*. Many of the July/August 1943 Jewish transportees were first held at Drancy transit camp outside Paris; Serge Klarsfeld identified one transportation to from Drancy to Alderney on 15 July 1943. This comprised 307 Jews, of whom 300 were *'Conjoint D'Aryenne*'.[225]

David Trat, then a 26 year old industrial designer was arrested in March 1943 in a round up of Jews and held at Drancy for four months before being transported by cattle wagon to Alderney via Cherbourg: '*It was madness then. The worst thing was that I was arrested by Frenchmen and held in Drancy by Frenchmen*'.

On arrival in Alderney the Jewish forced workers were sent to a special section of Norderney camp.[226] Trat remembered:

> '*I was part of the first batch of French internees to be sent to Alderney. Our task there was to build the island's concrete fortifications. We were put into a barracks where we slept on flea-infested mattresses. There were fleas and lice everywhere, in your hair even in your eyebrows. We tried to kill the insects when we could, before we went to bed, but we were exhausted.*'[227]

Albert Eblagon, grandson of the former Chief Rabbi of Crete, was a publisher's salesman prior to his arrest. He was transported to Alderney from France in August 1943: *'We arrived at night and disembarked on 15 August 1943, at three o'clock in the morning. In the darkness we were forced to run the two kilometres to Camp Norderney, while the German guards continuously stabbed into our backs with their bayonets while also kicking us all the time'*.[228] After the war Eblagon became President of 'Les Amicales des Anciens Deportees de Li'ile Anglo-Normande d'Aurigny', the Alderney survivors association.

Theodore Haenel was transported to Alderney on 1 October 1943. Born in Alsace-Lorraine, he and his family had been first deported to camps in southern France when their region was 'cleared' of Jews. Being fit and healthy he was selected for forced labour and sent to a camp in

[224] Theodore Haenel interview with author 9/10 May 1998.

[225] Klarsfeld, Le Calendrier de la persecution des Juifs de France, p.846.

[226] Norderney had been constructed with wooden barracks supplied by the Belgium firm De Cuhn of Courtrai and erected principally by Belgium workers.

[227] Trat stated that he had arrived in Alderney on 10 July 1943; he may therefore have been in of a different transportation than that noted by Klarsfeld.

[228] Steckoll, The Alderney Death Camp, p. 95.

Cherbourg in September 1943. He was then included in a transportation of around 400 Jews bound for Alderney. Of this transportation approximately 300 were *'Conjoint d'Aryenne'*. Haenels' family were transported to Auschwitz where they perished.[229]

Reuven Freidman, born in Lille, was arrested there in a round up of Jews by the French police and sent by train to Cherbourg in November 1943. On 17 December 1943, at the age of 17, he was included in a transportation of Jews bound for Norderney camp. Freidman testified:

> *'We arrived in the middle of the night, and didn't know where we were ... The officer of the camp took out his machine gun, put in on the table and began to read out the camp regulations. In addition to wearing the yellow patch, we had a white stripe the full length of our trousers on both sides ... In the camp there were about 800 Jews.'*[230]

Henri Uzan another Jewish forced labourer in Alderney, testified to French War crimes investigators in 1944:

> *'In August 1943, we were loaded onto boats with kicks and shouts. The Germans spat on us from the bridge above us. We stayed like that for twenty-four hours. It was a very rough crossing for everyone. A German, Heinrich Evers, greeted us with slaps, kicks and threats of his revolver. I was carrying two suitcases, and a soldier grabbed them from my hands. We had to march to the other end of the island. These were among us many who were more than sixty years old and who were ill. We were put to sleep in barracks without straw or blankets - only some dried leaves to sleep on. In the morning we discovered that we were covered with lice.*
>
> *All our luggage was taken except one blanket, one shirt, one pair of trousers and shoes. The German doctor came for twenty-five minutes to inspect four hundred men; he picked out the unfit. There was a quick interrogation by the German company*

---

[229] Haenel, interview with author, 9/10 May 1998; OT Bauleiter Ackerman confirmed under interrogation that 250 Jews and 150 'criminals' arrived at Norderney in Oct. 1943: see Pantcheff, Alderney Fortress Island, p. 9.

[230] Freidman testified that in addition to the Jews arrested in the round ups, other prisoners included black-marketeers, criminals and foreigners with inadequate registration papers Reuven Freidman, written testimony (Hebrew), Yad Vashem: One of the Guernsey fishermen interrogated by MI 19 in April 1944 stated 'The Jews wear ordinary civilian clothes with white stripes painted down the outside of their trouser legs. They also wear the yellow star on their left breast. The politicals [political prisoners referred to as 'Stripers'] wear blue and white striped prison garb like pyjamas. The coat, also striped, buttons up to the neck.' Other categories of workers were marked with a variety of coloured squares, letters, triangles and other markings. PRO WO 106/5248B

> *to which I had been assigned. They asked if I had any skills. I said I was a doctor, and the German just dictated to the secretary that I was a 'labourer, unskilled'. I was assigned to carry fifty kilos of cement. It was the same for a deputy, a famous lawyer, a pianist of world reputation, a lieutenant colonel.'*[231]

Kirill Nevrov, a non-Jewish prisoner at Norderney remembered the arrival of the Jewish forced workers:

> *'It happened just before we were taken to the Continent. There were a few Russians and Ukrainians left, most had died, but some had already been taken to France ... A few huts were separated from the rest by barbed wire. Special gates were made. It was a camp within a camp, designed specially for the Jews. They were fed separately. In front of the gate two barrels with paint were placed - one with white and the other with yellow paint. The white paint was used to renew the stripe on their trousers every day, the yellow, the star on their backs. Once the Russians noticed that the Jews were hiding something in the pile of wood lying beside one hut. Somebody managed to get there, and dug out golden rings, watches and other precious things. It was but natural to hide the jewellery; the Germans took everything away. Some of the dishonest people benefited at the expense of the Jews.'*[232]

Georgi Ivanovitch Kondakov recounted:

> *'Later on, already in France, I got into a camp situated close to the harbour [Cherbourg]. The first person I saw there was Levka Pilshikov dressed very stylishly. He had on a fine brown felt hat, a grey suit, a snow-white silk shirt with beautiful cuff-links, a tie and glittering black shoes with long narrow toes. I stared at him in a kind of shock. He looked like a cock on a fence. Looking at me with amusement, he told me that he had found a suitcase with all those fine clothes. It turned out that just before the Russians disembarked from Alderney, a group of Jews had arrived there. The Jews were ordered to leave all their things on the ground. They certainly obeyed, and were transported to the camp.*

---

[231] Bunting, The Model Occupation, p.183.

[232] Kirill Nevrov stated that in view of his appearance 'The Germans ... always wondered if I was a Jew', Georgi Kondakov, The Island of Dread in the Channel, (Stroud, 1991), pp. 98, 111.

> *Then the Russians arrived. Some of them also had baskets and suitcases that looked quite miserable in comparison with those standing on the quay. The quickest prisoners changed their poor cases for the rich ones. Levka was very quick and managed to take two suitcases at once, one of them was made of very good leather. It was in there that he discovered these wonderful clothes.'*[233]

Albert Eblagon recounted the appalling treatment he received:

> *'There were many men among us over seventy years of age but nobody was spared. Work, hard physical work for twelve and fourteen hours a day, every day, building the fortifications. Every day there were beatings and people's bones were broken, their arms or their legs. People died from overwork. We were starved and worked to death, so many died from total exhaustion.'*

David Trat remembered:

> *They would hit us on the shoulder with planks of wood, just to encourage us to work a little harder. One day I was in the hospital where I saw this man whose wrist had been broken in two places by a beating. He had still been forced to work with a shovel all day before being allowed to have treatment. But the worst thing was the hunger. I was always hungry, I felt as if I could eat non-stop. I was starving night and day. The staple diet was a clear soup, with the occasional small piece of beetroot or sausage and some bread. If you found something solid in your bowl, it was a real cause for celebration.*

Many other survivor accounts similarly detail the harsh treatment metered out to both Jewish and non-Jewish prisoners. One Norderney prisoner testified:

> *'Every day the Camp Commander made a habit of beating any man he found not standing properly to attention or who had not made his bed properly or did not execute a drill movement properly. The beatings were carried out on the head, face or body with a stick about 2 1/2 centimetres in diameter. The Camp Commander's assistant also beat workers daily with a stick of the same thickness on all parts of the body until their faces were covered with blood and they could not rise from the*

[233] Kondakov, The Island of Dread in the Channel, p.112.

> *ground, when he would call on the prisoner's mates to carry the prostrate body away.'*[234]

The Jewish section of Norderney camp was under the command of SS Untersurnführer/OT Hauptruppführer Adam Adler and OT Meister Heinrich Evers. Theodore Haenel remembered the camp being guarded by approximately a dozen men predominately recruited from '*Russian and Ukrainian*' units under German command.[235] Norbert Beernaert witnessed Heinrich Evers '*beat people to death many times*' and other survivor testimony and interrogation reports confirm his brutality.[236]

Three Russian OT workers imprisoned at Norderney stated to MI 19 interrogators in July 1944 '*The German camp guards beat ... [the forced workers] up pitilessly and for no reason. When the guards got drunk at night all the prisoners were dragged out of doors, paraded and beaten up with the handle shafts of pickaxes. This went on until the shaft broke. Many Russians died under the blows. Frequently the business end of the pickaxe was used.*[237]

Gordon Prigent, an 18 year old non-Jewish prisoner sent from Jersey to Alderney at the end of 1943, described daily life in Norderney:

> *'Roll call 06.00; marched to work on stone quarry, dock work or agricultural work; 12.00 - cabbage leaf soup and 1 slice of bread; 12.30 - back to work; 18.00 - march up to 3 miles back to Norderney; ladle of cabbage soup and 1 slice of bread; 19.15 - roll call; 20.00-23.00 - more work'*

Prigent detailed the barrack arrangements where workers slept on three tier bunks with only straw on wooden boards. Burials occurred on '*several days each week*'. He witnessed prisoners being whipped whilst

---

[234] Pantcheff, Alderney Fortress Island, p. 13.

[235] PRO WO 106/5248B (50157) confirms that 'Several Russians were employed as guards. These hand picked villains were sent to Paris for a special warder's course before being posted to a camp. They were armed with lengths of sand-filled rubber hosing with which they beat their wards unmercifully': Reuven Freidman stated that Adler would boast about being number 33 in the Nazi party. Freidman remembered well the commandant's brutality: Adam Adler ('General Allgemeine SS' not 'Deathshead SS'; Nazi Party number 330237) also held the rank of OT Hauptruppenführer: PRO WO 208/3629 confirms that Adler sometimes wore an SS uniform and at other times an OT uniform; Adler and Evers were tried at the Tribunal Militaire Permanent de Paris at Caserne de Reuilly in Sept. 1949 for subjecting Jews to 'superhuman work' and 'systematic ill-treatment'. For their crimes against Jews they were sentenced to ten and seven years imprisonment respectively.

[236] WO 106/5248B (2253), MI 19 Intelligence report, refers to Evers as 'the chief torturer of the Jews'..

[237] PRO WO 106/5248B (2376).

marching to and from work. Prigent's own teeth were knocked out when he was hit in the face with a rifle butt by a Norderney camp guard.[238]

The Basilov/Pantcheff report confirmed that *'workers were treated atrociously'*. The report detailed the regime at Norderney and Helgoland:

> *breakfast was half a litre of [ersatz] coffee without milk or sugar, lunch was half a litre of watery cabbage soup plus 1 kg of bread between 5-6 people. Two or three times a week 25gr of butter was distributed, very rarely, if at all, sausage, cheese or fresh vegetables, meat and sugar never ... foreign workers were not given any additional clothing in winter. Foreign workers worked 12 hours a day hard construction work. At midday there was a short break of 10-30 minutes. This regime continued 7 days a week ... only 1 Sunday a month they had a half day.*

Whilst food rations were poor for all workers, Jewish forced labourers received less food than other groups of workers.[239] Reuven Freidman testified that on occasional Sundays there was no work and on these days no food was issued. Like many other prisoners he contracted what became know amongst the prisoners as '*flea fever*'. Freidman was treated by a Jewish doctor named Rosenfeld and recovered.[240]

John Dalmau witnessed Jews working unloading boats: *'[the Jews] had reached such a degree of starvation that it was a pastime for the Germans to throw them pieces of carrot and see the pitiful wrecks fighting for it. The human part of the body appeared to be dead but the instinct for survival remained ... Cases of cannibalism were mentioned to me by an elderly Rumanian Jew ... Some of the octopuses and congers [caught whilst fishing] we gave to the Jews who ate them raw.'* [241]

Kirill Nevrov, referred to above, recounted the deprivations he suffered at Norderney:

---

[238] Taped interview with Gordon Prigent, Imperial War Museum; Prigent repeatedly referred to the guards at Norderney as being SS and those at the Soldatenheim as 'regular army'. He also stated that as the Allied invasion approached rumours circulated that the advancing Americans had shot a number of SS guards at a camp in France and in consequence the SS in Norderney changed their uniforms to those of the army and navy. He may have confused the SS uniforms with similar Ukrainian uniforms or he may have been referring to Adler's SS uniform.

[239] PRO file WO 106/5248B.

[240] Friedman stated that for accounting purposes the workers were technically paid RM 1 per day but that once a month this money was taken back from the prisoners.

[241] Bunting, The Model Occupation, p.183; During 'concrete pours' frequently work did not stop until the work was complete: Gordon Prigent, IWM interview: Dr J.M. Bloch another Jewish prisoner at Norderney stated to French investigators in 1944 that a number of work teams had to work sixty hour shifts with only twelve hours rest.

'We worked sometimes for as long as sixteen hours a day, building concrete walls around the island. Often we worked for twenty-four hours at a stretch, and we were then given half a day's rest before resuming work. My only wish was to rest; it was completely exhausting. I didn't even have the strength to move my hand. On one occasion we were working with the huge concrete-mixing machines and one man was so exhausted he lost his balance and slipped into the concrete. We told the German supervisor that someone had fallen in, but he said it was too complicated to stop the machine. It carried on pouring concrete over him. Many people died at the construction sites.[242]

After two or three months people started to die at the rate of about twelve men a day. There was a yard in the centre of the camp where people were shot for stealing cigarettes. In the morning many people were found dead in their beds, and the naked corpses were loaded into trucks. A truck would tip the corpses at low tide into pits dug in the beach fifty to a hundred metres off the shore. There would be about twelve people in each pit. You could never find the grave after the tide had been in and out because sand had been washed over it. I saw the bodies being buried with my own eyes, because I was working about fifty metres away on a concrete wall.

[Georgi] Kondakov and I have discussed many times why the corpses were naked. Perhaps it was because people came from work in clothes which were soaking wet, and they would take them off to sleep naked and then die in the night. We also took off our clothes to get some relief from the parasites at night. People stole blankets, but they wouldn't have bothered to steal clothes, because they were no more than rags.

I was nothing but skin and bones, and I had only the clothes I was wearing when they rounded me up in Russia the previous summer, which quickly fell apart. We made replacements out of old cement sacks; we cut off the corners to make holes for the arms and I used a rope as a belt. We used cement sacks for everything: blankets, leggings and even hats. We slept in cement powder because it was softer than our beds. We were covered in cement day and night and our hair got cemented.

[242] Albert Eblagon also witnessed the Germans throwing a fellow prisoner into the wet concrete: Interview with Solomon Steckoll. However, burial within the structure of the fortifications was not a usual method of disposal of prisoners.

> *There was nowhere to wash it off, but it did give us some protection against parasites. My trousers went so stiff with cement that when I took them off they remained standing. I used to be able to jump from my bunk into my standing trousers.*
>
> *Our huts were about thirty metres long, with men sleeping on either side on two levels of planks. At first it was one blanket per person, but after people began to die they gave us more blankets. When you lay down you fell asleep immediately; there was no time to feel cold. It was the sleep of a dead man.*
>
> *There was a passageway about one and half metres wide down the middle. At either end there were doors. There was a rail along the ceiling which the guards would beat with a hammer to wake everyone up. The last to leave the hut was beaten by the guards. We went to the canteen for breakfast, which was only a cup of herb tea that tasted of copper. There was about thirty minutes for lunch, which was cabbage soup; it only took a few minutes to drink it. Supper was more soup and bread. There was a one-kilogram loaf to share between seven people. The flour had been mixed with bonemeal and sawdust, so it wasn't like proper bread, and it was as hard as a brick. Occasionally we got 10-15 grams of margarine. Going to the toilet during work was a farce; a German guard would hold out the spade for me to do it on.*
>
> *... Alderney left a mark on the lives of all of us. Each time I go to bed or have a spare minute, I remember the things that happened on Alderney. I want people to know what it was like and to remember what happened.*'[243]

A German officer stationed in Alderney, despite claiming that the OT workers were '*voluntary*' labourers, described their suffering: '*I saw that they were vegetating under the most miserable conditions, really you couldn't call that living ... many of the labourers died through malnutrition weakness and exhaustion.*' He also confirmed that rations due to workers were stolen by their guards.[244]

Francisco Font was a former soldier in the Spanish Republican Army. Sent as a forced worker to Norderney he witnessed the Jewish prisoners in prayer:

> *'I remember watching how some of the Jewish prisoners would pray. They were not allowed to do this by the Germans. When*

[243] Bunting, The Model Occupation, p.165-7.
[244] Interview with Paul M., June 1990.

> *the barrack Kapo went to another hut to be together with the other Kapos, two men would stand at the doors at both sides of the hut. Then they would pray. Always, there were tears on their faces when they prayed. We used to watch it. This was on Saturdays, some Saturdays. Somehow they managed to put some cloth from shoulder to shoulder, some kind of sacramental thing. I don't know how they managed to keep it and hide it. This was the amazing thing. Somehow they managed also to have the black skull cap that they were not allowed to wear, which they put on their heads, you know, and after the praying was done they used to take it away and hide it, I don't know where. A lot of them joined in the praying and there were tears on their faces. I think their prayers were in Hebrew, as I could not understand the words. It was not French. The majority of them were older men. The younger ones sometimes used to join in but they were more casual.*
>
> *On Friday afternoons some lit candles ... I don't know where they found the candles or the matches, it was a mystery to everybody. They lit them on Friday night, very quiet, very secluded, with somebody standing guard at both doors, Jewish persons, while they had the little ceremony.*'[245]

Some of the Jewish forced workers were drawn towards their Jewish heritage whilst imprisoned in Alderney and Reuven Freidman recounted that he had given a talk to other Jewish prisoners about his dream of emigrating to Palestine after the war.[246]

The forced workers at Norderney were subjected to many terrors. Dr. H. Uzan, Dr J. Bloch, a French Jew, and Gordon Prigent each independently described how at the time of the Allied landings in France the prisoners of Norderney were forced to assemble in the 'Arch Bay' tunnel near the camp. A machine gun was trained on them and they were told they would be shot if the Allies landed in Alderney. Franz Doktor testified to war crimes investigators that '*all prisoners should be killed if Allied forces landed on Alderney*'. Josef Kranser provided similar testimony.[247]

---

[245] Steckoll, The Alderney Death Camp, p.87.

[246] Reuven Freidman emigrated from France to Israel in 1948.

[247] Prigent, taped interview, Imperial War Museum and The Observer, 1981; Basliov/Pantcheff report , Moscow State Archives.

The transportation of many of the Jewish forced workers from Norderney, destined for Neuengamme.

In early April 1944 the German command in Paris signed an order effectively inaugurating the final stage of the deportation of Jews from France. All Jews of French nationality were to be seized, only the '*Conjoint D'Aryennes*' were to be spared deportation to death camps. Even they were to be sent to OT camps to replace Jews who had been deported. In this final phase More than 6,000 Jews were deported from mainland France mainly to Auschwitz-Birkenau.[248]

As the Allied invasion of German occupied Europe became evident the Germans planned the transportation of the Jewish forced workers at Norderney to Neuengamme concentration camp.

OT Haupttruppführer Johann Hoffman stated '*In Norderney Camp almost all the Russians were withdrawn between September-October 1943 and January 1944. In June 1944, after the invasion, all the Jews, Frenchmen and Moroccans were evacuated.*'[249]

The International Red Cross have records of two groups of Jews and North Africans, each of around 200 men, '*transferred from Norderney Camp to an unknown destination because they were unable to work*' in January and March 1944.[250]

Serge Klarsfeld recorded the arrival of 39 Jewish forced workers from Alderney at Saint-Lo (Manche) via the Hospice Rothschild on 19 January 1944. Klarsfeld recorded another transport of 97 Jews from Alderney, arriving at Drancy transit camp via the Picpus annex on 17 April.

Other Jews from Alderney already being held at the Picpus annex were ordered for transfer to Drancy on 14 July in order to establish whether they were fully Jewish or '*Conjoints d'Aryenne*'; those categorised as the former were designated for onward transportation to concentration camps. In a statement made after liberation an administrator at Picpus claimed that he had prevented the transfer of three ex-Alderney Jewish forced labourers to Drancy. He claimed that three transportees,

---

[248] The order to transport the remaining French Jews was signed by Bds Standartenführer Knochen and Hauptstrumführer Brunner on 14 April 1944

[249] Capt. T. Pantcheff 'Official British government report about the atrocities on Alderney', Moscow State Archives; Pantcheff, Alderney Fortress Island, p. 9.

[250] Steckoll, The Alderney Death Camp, p.104; Gordon Prigent estimated that as the allied invasion of France approached around 300 of the 1,000 prisoners still at Norderney were transported from Alderney: Imperial war Museum, taped interview with Prigent.

Solomonvitch, Moskowitz and Kous, had been in danger of being categorised as full Jews.[251]

The main transportation of around 800 Norderney Jews left Alderney on 6/7 May 1944. David Trat, Reuven Freidman and Theodore Heanel were included in this convoy. They were put in cattle wagons at Cherbourg on a train routed initially to Boulogne and destined for Neuengamme concentration camp.

David Trat persuaded a railway worker to give him a hammer and chisel, which he used to cut a hole in the floor of the wagon. He dropped through the hole down onto the track: '*My companion was injured jumping onto the track and was spotted and picked up by the Germans. I just lay there on the track underneath the wagon until the train moved on*'. Trat succeeded in making his way back to Paris.

Theodore Haenel remained on the train on a journey that lasted 13 days in locked cattle wagons with little water. The railway lines were frequently bombed and the train was shunted backwards and forwards as the Germans attempted to find a railway route to Neuengamme. A number of prisoners attempted to escaped between Cherbourg, Lille and Hazebrouck. Some succeeded in their escape, those recaptured were shot.[252]

The train stopped at Hazebrouck where the older prisoners taken to an interment camp at the Marette school in Boulogne. The younger prisoners were transported to Dannes work camp near Camiers where they were put to work repairing damaged German coastal fortifications in the Boulogne-Calais-Dunkerque area.

In early September 1944, in a final effort to transport the Jews to Neuengamme they were forced to march for three days before being put once again on a train. On 4 September 1944 the convoy arrived at Diksmuide in Belgium. When the Belgium resistance realised that the transportation comprised Jews destined for Neuengamme, they blew up the railway line leading out of the town to prevent the train travelling further. The Belgium resistance ordered the German train guards to release the prisoners and a number of Red Cross representatives assisted the weak Jewish prisoners. The residents of Diksmuide co-operatively

[251] Schendel report, Centre de Documentation Juive Contemporaine, primarily detailing the final round up of Jewish children in France; Bds Standartenfuhrer Knochen and Hauptstrumfuhrer Brunner had ordered that a special watch must be kept on Jews sent to Drancy. A number had escaped in earlier transportations and they recommended that Jews be tied to one another with a long rope.

[252] Theodore Haenel, interview with author, 9/10 May 1998: Notes prepared by Colin Partridge, entitled 'The War of 1939-1945- Historical Facts on Alderney'.

cared for the Jews, providing them with shelter, food and clothing until the town was liberated by the Canadian forces a few days later.[253]

The transportation of most of the remaining Alderney forced workers on 24 June 1944

In December 1943 most of the prisoners in Sylt had been transported back to the French mainland. A change of policy however resulted in the return of the majority to Alderney only a few weeks later. By early April 1944 groups of Sylt prisoners were being transported back to mainland Europe.[254]

On 24 June 1944, after D-Day, the Germans finally began the mass evacuation of most of the SS Sylt prisoners together with many workers from other Alderney camps. Cherbourg had been cut off by the advancing Allies and the prisoners, including the remaining Jewish forced labourers, accompanied by SS guards and personnel from Sylt concentration camp were transported to Guernsey and Jersey. After a few days they were transported on to the French port of St Malo.[255]

The Reverend Douglas Ord recorded the arrival of the transportation of Sylt prisoners in Guernsey:

> *'25 June 1944 - we heard a curious shuffling sound as of many feet in sabots. We went down the drive to the gates and there we saw a dreadful sight. Coming down from the harbour was a column of men in rows of five. All were in striped pyjama suits of sorts and their footgear varied from wooden sabots ... to pieces of cloth bound round the feet. Others were barefoot. There were more than the 1000 of them – political prisoners brought away from Alderney and being fetched down by their guards to an open field at Blanc Bois. They were shaven-head and in varying degrees of weariness or lameness ... Scattered thorough the column among men of sub-human criminal type were others obviously intellectuals, men of superior calibre who*

---

[253] Klarsfeld, Le Calendrier 1995 and Theodore Haenel, interview with author, 9/10 May 1998. Haenel escaped from Dannes work camp on 1 Sept. 1944; Freidman testimony, Yad Vashem: Freidman stated that the Belgium resistance would have stormed the train under cover of night if the German guards had not agreed to an early release.

[254] PRO WO 106/5248B and WO 199/2090A; OT Bauleiter Leo Ackerman stated to investigators that the prisoners at SS Sylt were first transported back to France in December 1943 however after three weeks a reduced number were returned to Alderney, Capt. T. Pantcheff 'Official British government report about the atrocities on Alderney', Moscow State Archives; Dutch Red Cross records, see Steckoll P.96

[255] PRO WO 199/3303 Robert Prokop a Czech who had both been transported to Sylt in March 1943 testified that the evacuation of Sylt camp on 24 June 1944 comprised 527 prisoners

> *had offended the brutal Nazi regime. It tore the heart to see the effects of this systematic and deliberate degradation of human beings. At the head of the column marched five evil-visaged SS men armed with automatic guns. At the rear of the column and along its flanks on both sides and at a distance of about a dozen feet from each other were more of these brutes, similarly armed, and all on alert for any attempt at a break-away. I have never seen such brutality written on human countenances ... Occasionally a man would make the 'V' sign to us as he went by. All the emotions of pity, sympathy, sorrow, anger and horror surged through us as we watched ... All day long the stench of their poor, wretched, unwashed bodies and clothes hung about the route they had* followed.'

On the following day Reverend Douglas Ord noted the arrival of the workers from other Alderney camps:

> *'26 June 1944 - After breakfast we had to witness another sorry column – about 1,400 strong – of degraded human beings coming up from the harbour. This time they were a marvellous lot of foreign workers of all races as it seemed ... Their impoverished clothing was beyond description, while some had scarcely rags enough to cover their naked bodies.*
>
> *27 June 1944 - Town was full of all kinds of foreign workmen and Germans obviously back form Alderney, or possibly even from Cherbourg ... Twelve boats left harbour last night. The prisoners were taken away together with the foreign women (camp followers for the most part)'.*

Leslie Sinel recorded the arrival in Jersey of the prisoners including many of the remaining Jewish forced workers:

> *'28 June 1944 – In the morning six fair sized vessels, with an escort, arrived with 1,500 persons of all nationalities. It was learned that they were foreign workers from Alderney, prisoners from a concentration camp in that Island, a few evacuees from Cherbourg and some foreign workers from Guernsey, military and naval personnel also arrived, as well as Jerseymen who had been working in Alderney. The prisoners were taken under armed escort to Fort Regent; some were in a pitiable state, and many were garbed in a blue and white striped uniform - Jews, Poles, Russians, and even German political prisoners. There were many Frenchmen among them, and it was estimated that about half the number from Alderney was taken to the Fort. The others, including many women, were*

> *lodged at some of the larger hotels, and quantities of mattresses and blankets were taken into West Park Pavilion. During the day these people swarmed all over the town and German armed guards were posted outside cafe entrances. About 8.00 p.m. all the morning's arrivals were taken to the harbour to be taken on to France, but, after waiting about, they were sent back to their billets as it was found that the weather was too rough. Many local people congregated near the harbours, and, when the guards were not looking threw cigarettes to the men who, in reply, gave the V-sign. The guards treated them very roughly, and harrowing tales of life in the Alderney concentration camp have been told by local workers who returned from that Island.'* [256]

The ex-Alderney forced workers were transported back to occupied France in a number of convoys. Sinel noted one attempt to transport the '*Foreign workers*' to France on the evening of 29 June. They were unable to embark and were '*taken back to their billets or to the Fort Regent prison...at night [30 June] they embarked again, and this time the boats went by a different route – some by the eastern and others by the western passage. They reached their destination except for one vessel which ran aground between here and St Malo and was forced to return.*'[257]

In another covey on the night of 3 July 1944, approximately 500 workers, including a number of Jewish forced workers, were loaded onto the *SS Minotaure.* The convoy, escorted by four escort vessels came under Allied attack. Denis Le Cuirot a Jersey hospital worker who had stowed away on the *Minotaure* recounted the tragedy to Military Intelligence: '*[British MTB's ordered the] convoy to stop. The Germans refused to stop and tried to run ... In a quarter of an hour the four escort vessels were sunk and we had a torpedo in the bows and a shell aft*'. After the war Le Cuirot stated '*of the 500 passengers about half lost their lives when the crowded ship was hit*'.[258]

On 24 July one convoy of 300 ex-Sylt prisoners and 30 SS guards arrived at Tours, where they were forced to clear unexploded bombs. On 26 July

---

[256] Leslie Sinel, 'The German Occupation of Jersey. A Complete Diary of Events June 1940-June 1945', Jersey Evening Post, 1945. Fort Regent was the site where many of the early Jewish forced workers brought to Jersey in 1941-2 had been held.

[257] The log book of the German ship Gerfreid confirms the dates of some convoys of those evacuated from Alderney to Guernsey, Jersey and finally France, arriving in St Malo at 09.50 on 1 July 1944, Pantcheff, Alderney Fortress Island, p. 37.

[258] Jersey Evening Post June 1945:A number of accounts have stated that all the workers on the Minotaure were Jews. However, although there were undoubtedly a number of Jewish forced workers on the Minotaure the majority of the transportees on the ship were non-Jews.

eighteen prisoners were shot by the SS at Breuvannes as they attempted to escape. Other died at Rennes. Jan Woitas, a Polish ex-Sylt prisoner described the punishment administered to two prisoners recaptured after an escape attempt at Rennes:

> *'Several Russians were bound hand and foot and were beaten so hard that by the evening they were dying. Wolf returned in the evening and hit the three boys with the butt of his rifle until they fainted. Then he pumped them with bullets. They stayed 24 hours in the truck with us.'*

Ex-Sylt prisoners were transported, via Lyons, to Kortemark in Belgium where they laboured on the V1/2 construction sites before being moved to Sollstedt, a satellite camp of Buchenwald, in Germany.

As the Allied forces neared, a convoy of ex-Sylt prisoners were transported via Kladrav Pilsen, Katowice and, Budweis to Mauthausen concentration camp. In May 1945 in a final attempt to prevent their liberation, the Germans marched the ex-Sylt prisons out of Mauthausen in one of the final death marches of the war. However the American army were only a few miles away and on 5 May 1945 the survivors were liberated at Remingsdorf-Steyr.[259]

Worker deaths

The conditions experienced by all forced workers were extremely harsh, brutality was commonplace and many died from disease, starvation, overwork and beatings. Workers were subjected to 'hard labour' however, the camps in Alderney were not 'mass extermination' camps of the form of Auschwitz-Birkenau, Treblinka or Sobibor. Consequently worked out forced labourers were returned to mainland Europe. Many perished in other work camps, concentration camps and extermination centres in mainland Occupied Europe.

Reverend Ord and Deputy Le Quesne had both witnessed worked-out labourers being returned to France. Gordon Prigent estimated that forced workers were so starved and incapable of work, they only lasted in Alderney for around nine months before their onward transportation.

---

[259] Solomon Steckoll The Alderncy Death Camp P.83, Madeleine Bunting, The Model Occupation, London 1995, P. 189, testimony of Wilhelm Wernegau; At Toul a monument records 'Here are buried seventeen victims of Nazi brutality – July 1944': PRO WO 199/3303 interrogation reports of Leonid Winogradow, a Russian radio engineer previously an inmate of Sachsenhausen concentration camp and Robert Prokop a Czech who had both been transported to Sylt in March 1943; Maj T Pantcheff stated that the prisoners were renamed SS Baubrigade 5 in Germany: Solomon Steckoll, The Alderney Death camp P.96; Brian Bonnard, Alderney at War, P.70

Before the evacuation of Alderney in 1944 transportations of 'worked out' prisoners had taken place from Sylt to Neuengamme. One transportation left Alderney in July 1943 comprising 200 prisoners suffering from '*festering sores, TB and dysentery*' and according to SS Obersturmführer Kurt Klebeck '*not working and ... thus useless.*' SS Hauptsturmführer Maximilian List stated that he had ordered their transportation to Neuengamme concentration camp for '*extermination*'. They were so weak that by the time they left Cherbourg on 6 July 1943 50 were already dead.[260]

The approximately 450 identified foreign worker graves in Alderney, 140 in Jersey and 120 in Guernsey do not represent the total of those who died in the Island, however the exact figure is unlikely ever to be known.[261] As the cost of the burial of workers was usually the responsibility of the contracting firm to whom they had been assigned many workers were buried where they fell. Many dead workers were thrown into the sea. V.I. Rosslova testified: '*A lorry loaded with corpses would go to the end of the breakwater which stuck out 500 meters into the bay, dumped its horrible load and came back.*' Georgi Kandakov, and T. Misiewicz also each independently record having seen bodies of prisoners being thrown off the Alderney breakwater. John Dalmau testified that when he dived near the breakwater '*among the rocks and seaweed there were skeletons all over the place*'.[262] Kirill Nevrov and Ivan Sholomitsky both independently stated that they had seen prisoners buried in the sand at low tide.

Johann Burbach, a German engineer in Alderney told British interrogators in 1945 that he had seen corpses being transported across the Island; '*they were completely emaciated consisting of skin and bones*'[263] Otto Tauber stated to war crimes investigators '*I often saw corpses on the street [in the winter of 1942/3] people were dying from*

[260] An attempted escape occurred during this transportation. In consequence List and Klebeck were court-martialed. They were acquitted their Nov. 1943 Berlin trial records have survived: Berlin Document Centre; Steckoll, The Alderney Death Camp, pp.167-71.

[261] Brian Bonnard identified 437 graves but estimated the total deaths in Alderney exceeded this figure, Conversation with author, 25 April 1998.

[262] V.I.Rosslova also stated that OT Frontführer Lucian Linke stopped this practice as 'Russian corpses were littering the sea.': Account by Georgi Kondakov, Alderney magazine, 1989; T. Misiewicz stated 'I frequently saw how the dead were carried, several in a box and dumped into the harbour. That box was used over and over again'; Grenadier Walter Schuller under interrogation confirmed that he had seen false bottomed coffins in use: PRO WO 208/3629; After the war a reusable two man false bottomed coffin was found in Alderney by the British forces. Dalmau stated that bodies were sometimes weighted down with stones: Dalmau, Slave Worker, p.19; Pantcheff, Alderney Fortress Island, p.85

[263] Bunting, The Model Occupation, p. 289; Daily Telegraph, 20 Nov. 1996.

hunger. I saw corpses so thin, you could see the outline of their ribs. I saw 12 corpses completely naked'.[264]

Dr Anthony Glees, the Home Office advisor on war crimes stated '*I should be surprised if the numbers killed by the Nazis [in Alderney] did not run into thousands.*' One British Intelligence report stated: '*during the informants [18 month] stay on the island, out of 2000 Russian labourers 843 died, very few of them from natural causes*'. A MI 19 interrogation report of July 1944 estimated that of the 1,600 'Russians' transported to Alderney between April and August 1942 around half had died through undernourishment and exhaustion. The Basilov/Pantcheff report confirms that the total number of deaths likely substantially exceeds the identified graves.[265]

John Dalmau testified that political prisoners and Jews were shot especially after Allied raids on German towns:

> *'The news of any heavy bombing of German towns was the occasion for a 'dance'. Organised by the SS, the 'dance' consisted of gathering 50 or more political prisoners or Jews and making them jump, firing bullets at their feet. When one was hit and fell, another bullet, this time in the head, finished him off. This frightful affair continued until the last man fell.'*

Otto Spehr, a worker in Alderney between June 1943 and June 1944 confirmed that SS Hauptsturmfüher Maximilian List and Lagerfuhrer Puhr had ordered the shooting of many workers.[266]

Some workers in Alderney were thrown into mass graves. Prekshatt, a German who had worked under Commandant Zuske stated '*a truck collected the naked corpses which were taken off the truck with pitchforks and thrown into a general grave*'. Major Pantcheff confirmed '*two multiple shootings accounting for nearly 50 prisoners in all*'.

---

[264] Otto Tauber was in Alderney Dec. 1940-Jan. 1945: Capt. T. Pantcheff 'Official British government report about the atrocities on Alderney', Moscow State Archives.

[265] Dr Glees estimated that in total 16,000 workers were brought into Alderney during the Occupation, Bonnard, Alderney at War, p. 78; PRO WO 106/5248B (2376); One witness Brian O'Hurley stated that 700 had died over the winter of 1942/43 alone. The surviving prisoners estimated that as many as 3,220 died excluding those who died under the SS at Sylt and those lost on the Minotaure: Steckoll, The Alderney Death Camp, p.104; Capt. T. Pantcheff 'Official British government report about the atrocities on Alderney', Moscow State Archives; George Pope stated to war crimes investigators that in 1942 two thousand Ukrainians arrived of whom 1,778 died. Alan and Mary Wood, Islands in Danger, p.162 stated that George Pope had claimed to have a record of 1,000 deaths in Alderney which he failed to present to investigators when requested to do so. The 'Official British government report about the atrocities on Alderney' at the Moscow State Archives also casts doubt on the reliability of Pope as a witness; PRO WO 199/2090B-50157, MI 19 Interrogation report on a number of Russians brought back from Cherbourg by the Allies in 1944.

[266] WO 199/3303 Report on MI 19 interrogation of Otto Spehr, 13 Dec. 1944

Solomon Steckoll recounted that British forces uncovered two mass graves in Alderney in May 1945, containing 83 and 48 bodies. The British forces erected a memorial over the latter: '*Here lie forty-eight unknown Soviet Citizens who died during the German Occupation 1941-1945*'. Rev. Ord also witnessed forced workers being interred at Foulon cemetery in Guernsey '*several in each grave*'[267]

As was the case at German concentration camps throughout occupied Europe, the lists of the causes of death at the Sylt camp were often purposely misleading. The remaining death certificates provide little useful indication of the 'real' causes of death. Verwaltungsoberinspektor Hans Spann stated:

> '*When a foreign worker died, the OT Frontfuhrung sent a copy of the death certificate ... It was already my opinion at that time that not too much reliability could be attached to such a certificate ... I was struck by the disorder [in the cemetery] and marked lack of dignity with which the corpses had been buried ... I am extremely doubtful if the names on the individual graves were correct*'. The clerk to the Fortress doctor in 1944 stated '*The death certificates of Sylt camp consisted of a printed form on which the cause of death, which was always heart failure or faulty circulation, was typed in. The cause of death was filled in by the SS. The death certificate was then presented to the Fortress Doctor for signature.*'[268]

Major Pantcheff stated:

> '*the German records in Alderney were so confusing that one cannot but doubt whether those traditionally so renowned for meticulous and efficient administration were in this instance really aiming at clarity. There are death certificates, sometimes manifestly misleading; there are executive reports, which do not always tally with the certificates; there are names on crosses, out of chronological sequence, in nine cases bearing two different names on the same grave with one body, and in 22 cases marking two graves in different places with the same*

[267] Capt. T. Pantcheff 'Official British government report about the atrocities on Alderney', Moscow State Archives, testimony of 'Perkshatt'; In Guernsey Rev. Ord diary entries 29 Jan. 1942 and 16 Nov. 1942; The 'Official British government report about the atrocities on Alderney' at the Moscow State Archives states that investigators had found 58 graves on the north side of St Annes Church, the majority marked with a cross. Most were 'Russian' with five French and Dutch graves. A memorial plaque was placed in the north wall of St Anne's church inscribed '1941-1945 – near this place are buried 45 Soviet citizens who died in Alderney. Their names are recorded in the States Office'

[268] Capt. T. Pantcheff 'Official British government report about the atrocities on Alderney', Moscow State Archives; Pantcheff, Alderney Fortress Island, pp. 66, 68.

names and dates of birth ... Some were reported dead but with no known grave marked with their name'.

Even the graves of those who had been buried in the Alderney forced worker cemeteries were desecrated by Germans. War crimes investigators received testimony confirming that crosses had been torn up and burnt and the ground levelled.[269]

The identified Jewish graves

As previously stated, the exact number of Jewish forced workers who died either in the Channel Islands or after their transportation back to the occupied European mainland is unlikely to ever be known.

OT Bauleiter Leo Ackermann who had arrived in Alderney on 20 August 1943 admitted under interrogation that '*several*' of the 250 Jews and 150 '*criminals*' who arrived during his administration in October 1943 had died as a result of the *'incurable diseases they had brought with them'*.[270]

Eight graves containing the remains of Jewish forced workers transported to Alderney in May-December 1943 were identified after the war buried in the north-west corner of Longis Common. In 1945 the British Army erected a board adjacent to the graves inscribed '*Here lie the bodies of eight French nationals of the Jewish faith who died during the German Occupation 1941-1945*'. The graves were marked with individual plaques in the form of the two conjoined tablets of the 'ten commandments' inscribed with the deceased's name.

The following are the eight identified Jewish graves::

Robert Perlestein, died 22 Dec 1943
Lucien Worms, died 7 Jan 1944
Wilfred Gordesson, died 26 Feb 1944
Chaim Goldin, died 7 Dec 1943
Seib Becker, died 30 Dec 1943
Henri Lipmann, died 2 Mar 1944
Isaac Streskoski, died 8 Feb 1944

---

[269] Testimony given to war crimes investigators stated that 'Richta' had torn up and burnt crosses of workers in the cemetery and levelled the ground: Capt. T. Pantcheff 'Official British government report about the atrocities on Alderney', Moscow State Archives.

[270] Capt. T. Pantcheff 'Official British government report about the atrocities on Alderney', Moscow State Archives

Shmuel Kirszenblat, died 26 Apr 1944

Theodore Haenel noted that the names of two of the Jewish forced workers at Norderney known to him to have died in Alderney do not appear in this list. One an 18 year old was killed when a container of concrete fell on his head.[271]

The remains of Robert Perlestein, Lucien Worms and Wilfred Gordesson were exhumed and reburied by their families prior to 1961. However under an agreement between the Allies and the Federal Republic of Germany in 1959 it was decided that the dead forced workers should be '*counted to the German war dead*'. Thus along with the remains of other forced workers who had died in Alderney the bodies of the five remaining Jewish forced workers were exhumed by the 'Volksbund Deutscher Kreigsgraberfursorge' (German War Graves Commission) and reburied at Mont de Huisnes German Military Cemetery at La Manche, France in 1961.

'Les Amicales des Anciens Deportees' naturally raised strong objection to the burial of the five Jewish forced workers in a German military cemetery and consequently on 19 May 1963 the bodies of Chayim Goldin, Seib Becker, Henri Lipmann, Isaac Streskoski and Shmuel Kirszenblat were reburied at the Cimatiere de Saint Ouen, Seine-St Denis in one vault in the 36th division North, 1st row North No. 25.

War-crimes investigations

Investigations concerning the perpetrators of war-crimes against foreign forced workers followed an unproductive path.

In July 1943 Jersey labourers returning from periods of work in Alderney had brought back eye-witness accounts of the atrocities committed there against Jews and Russians. In April 1944 Guernsey labourers provided similar accounts.

By March 1944 '*awful tales*' of atrocities in German concentration camps on the European mainland were circulating in the Islands. The Germans printed propaganda articles in the Jersey Evening Post refuting these rumours.

Reverend Ord in Guernsey heard stories specifically relating to the mistreatment of Jewish forced workers in Alderney. He noted in his diary

[271] Theodore Haenel estimated that approximately 10-12 Jews from the Jewish camp at Norderney died during the period Oct. 1943-May 1944 but added that others died after they left Alderney: Interview with author, 9/10 May 1998. Reuven Freidman provided similar testimony.

on 16 April 1944 *'Jews received negligible rations. They are forced to work from 5am to 10 pm, or till they dropped. One of them fainted in a field. The Germans drove the plough-tractor over him.'*

Within a few days of the end of the war reports of atrocities in Alderney appeared in the national British press.[272]

Many of those who had subjected prisoners to mistreatment including OT Bauleiter Leo Ackermann and OT Johann Hoffmann fell into British hands in 1945, but they were released without formal charge.[273]

The initial enthusiasm for war crimes prosecutions waned when the British government realised that as most of the victims of the atrocities in Alderney had been Russian, the Soviet Union would have to mount any trial.

The only war crimes trials specifically relating to the mistreatment of Jews by Germans in the Channel Islands took place at Caserne de Reuilly, France in September 1949. SS Untersurnführer/OT Hauptruppführer Adam Adler and OT Meister Heinrich Evers, the commandant and deputy commandant of the Jewish camp at Norderney were sentenced to ten and seven years imprisonment respectively for subjecting French Jews to '*superhuman work*' and '*systematic ill-treatment*'.

Memorials to the Forced Workers

A memorial plaque in Hebrew to the Jewish forced workers who perished in Alderney is included in the Hammond Memorial near Longis Common. This memorial plaque was established at the instigation of Mr Alfred Herzka of London and unveiled by Cpt. S. Herivel, CBE, DSC, President of the States of Alderney on 13 August 1969. Prayers were led by Rabbi E. Gastwirth as the representative of the Chief Rabbi. A delegation from the Jersey Jewish Congregation attended both the dedication and many subsequent annual services.

---

[272] 'The Occupation of Jersey Day by Day – The personal diary of Deputy Edward Lee Quesne', La Haule Books, Jersey 1999, entry 20-24 July 1943; Rev. D. Ord diary, 16 April 1944; Jersey Evening Post, 4 March 1944; Articles had recently appeared in the British national newspapers. Typically, 'Huns whip slaves to death on British soil' the Daily Mirror 23 Feb 1944 detailed the mistreatment of forced workers in Guernsey.

[273] In 1949 a Russian was sentenced to 25 years hard labour for war crimes committed whilst a Kapo in Alderney. SS Lagerfuhrer Puhr who had served in Alderney was executed in 1963 in East Germany for war crimes not specifically committed in Alderney; Johann Hoffmann who arrived in Alderney in Jan. 1943 was Commandant of Helgoland; Maj. Carl Hoffmann had been Island Commander July 1941-Dec. 1941 and remained in the Island until Nov. 1943: see Capt. T. Pantcheff 'Official British government report about the atrocities on Alderney', Moscow State Archives and PRO Home Office files HO144/45.

At Westmount, St Helier, Jersey a memorial to the forced workers who perished in the Island was established initially incorporating just a plaque to the Russian workers. However other plaques were subsequently added recognising Spanish, French and Polish workers.

In 1998 the Jersey Jewish Congregation with the consent of the States of Jersey added a plaque to the Westmount memorial dedicated to Jewish forced workers who suffered in all the Channel Islands. This plaque reads '*To the Jews who suffered during the Occupation 1940-1945*'. An annual memorial service is held at the Westmount memorial on Liberation day.

Perhaps however, the most poignant memorials to the suffering of Jewish forced workers in the Islands is the simple 'Star of David' cut by a Jewish forced labourer into the shuttering of a German bunker in Alderney together with the yellow 'Star of David' clothing badges marked 'Jude' and 'Juif' found in Alderney and Sark.[274]

[274] The forced worker Stars of David are on display at the Guernsey Occupation Museum and the Sark Occupation and Heritage Museum.

Index